FESTING — FIELD MARSHAL

A Study of 'Front Line Frankie',
G.C.B., K.B.E., D.S.O.

Admiral Mountbatten and Major-General Festing on the North bank of Shweli River during a bombing attack, February 1945.

Also by Lyall Wilkes

Tyneside Classical (with Gordon Dodds) (John Murray 1964)
Tyneside Portraits Studies in Art and Life (Frank Graham 1971)
John Dobson, Architect and Landscape Gardener (Oriel Press and Routledge 1980)
South and North and Other Poems (Oriel Press 1983)
The Aesthetic Obsession (Routledge 1985)
A Portrait of Sir William Eden Bt.

FESTING — FIELD MARSHAL

A Study of 'Front Line Frankie', G.C.B., K.B.E., D.S.O.

Lyall Wilkes

BG

The Book Guild Ltd
Sussex, England

The Book Guild Limited
25 High Street
Lewes, Sussex

First published 1991

Set in Baskerville
Typeset by Hawks Phototypesetters Ltd
Copthorne, West Sussex
Printed in Great Britain by
Antony Rowe Ltd
Chippenham, Wiltshire

British Library Cataloguing In Publication Data
Wilkes, Lyall
Festing — Field-Marshal: a study of 'Front Line Frankie'.
1. World War, 1939-1945. Campaigns
I. Title
940.548141

ISBN 086332 532 7

For all those who served with Frankie Festing, especially the members of the 29th Brigade who captured Madagascar, and the men of the 36th Division who helped to break the Japanese hold on Burma.

'There is too much talk of the futility of war. The only truly futile war is the war you lose. The wars we have won have at least kept the way open for a civilised way of life.'

Asked whether he preferred working under a Labour or Conservative Government, he replied, 'Definitely under Labour, for under Labour the Minister of Defence will very likely be an ex-lance corporal who knows nothing and knows he knows nothing, and will be prepared to accept military advice, whereas in a Conservative Government the Minister of Defence will probably be an ex-Major from some pretty ineffectual Yeomanry Regiment and thinks he knows it all.'

'The world is full of boring jobs and boring people do them best.'

CONTENTS

INTRODUCTION

This is a study of one of the most distinguished soldiers of the Second World War, a soldier whose bravery and uninhibited commonsense set him apart in his rise to the very peak of his profession.

When Field Marshal Festing died in 1976, Lieutenant-General Sir John Cowley wrote[1].

'It is greatly to the credit of the British Army that a man of such great qualities and such a fine disregard for the details which some officers consider so important should have reached the top.'

A huge man, six feet four inches tall, with untidy ginger hair he had a taste in dress and uniform which was unconventional to say the least. An ADC was heard to complain that on parade Festing frequently reminded him of an unmade bed. One of the best-loved and certainly the least conventional of all Field Marshals, he was a man who clearly agreed with Samuel Johnson that 'it is not necessary to be grave to be serious.'

His bravery in action was only equalled by his determination in war to see for himself everything that affected the welfare and safety of the ordinary soldier whom he championed all his life; but in peacetime he favoured, in his own words, 'the maximum of encouragement and the minimum of interference'. His giant ash walking stick, used like a Highland shepherd's crook, was carried by him everywhere and has an honourable place in British military history, the citation for his D.S.O. earned in Madagascar in

1. *The Times* 14th August 1976

1942 recording, 'He was always an inspiration and forceful, as on the occasion when he applied his walking stick to the backsides of the few recalcitrants who appeared to have an unnecessary interest in the rear areas.'

He was even seen chasing Jap snipers with it. An American correspondent described him as: 'The kind of man who would have walked gleefully with Robin Hood or Friar Tuck'. Festing, with Montgomery and Slim, were the three wartime British generals that 'Vinegar Joe' Stilwell considered the best in action.

His other talent, second only in importance to his bravery, was his ability, when presented with a problem, quickly to put his finger on the nub of it and to provide the right answer. Like a first-rate lawyer he had the capacity to separate the relevant from the irrelevant and to be able to reduce an apparently extremely complicated problem to its essential simplicities which could be stated in a few sentences. This capacity was all the more remarkable in that he refused to read much — 'He did not seem to need to,' said his Under Secretary at the War Office, the Right Hon James Ramsden. His ADC at Eastern Command, Paul Greenwood, said, 'He used to worry me by not reading his brief until very shortly before a meeting but he was invariably able to resolve the matter quickly and accurately.' Partly because of his extremely blunt speech he had his detractors, but his popularity with the troops and with regimental officers never wavered.

His name will always be associated with his famous 36th Division of the 14th Army which helped to break the Japanese stranglehold on Burma by chasing the Japanese army out of the railway corridor from Myitkina to Katha, and in a ten month campaign covering over 700 miles of jungle, mud and swamp, crossing the Irrawaddy and Shweli rivers to Kalaw, opened up the road to Mandalay and to the recapture of Rangoon by 15 Corps on 3rd May 1945.

Whitehall with its committees, civil servants, and politics was not to his liking at all, although contrary to his bluff appearance and speech he could be a subtle in-fighter in diplomacy as well as war, as the Chinese found in 1945 and again in 1949, and the Egyptians from 1952-54. Soldiering to him was primarily training and leading men, and if he could not do that then the next best thing was to breathe in the air of the wide open spaces of Northumberland.

When he was appointed, not very imaginatively, to be G.O.C. Eastern Command in 1954 he addressed his Chief of Staff[2] as follows — 'I do not like this part of England and I will be away most of the time . . . when I am away, you make all the decisions without referring to me. When I return, if the War Office questions your decisions, I will tell them that you are right and they are wrong — but I may not always tell you that and if you continue to make decisions that I consider wrong, I will find another Chief of Staff.'

This was an example of how his philosophy of 'the maximum of encouragement with the minimum of interference' was carried out in practice. His other great principle was 'always to lead from the front, to show your men you are not afraid to go any place you order them to go. A commander must get out amongst his men. Even if they don't like him it is better to get that reaction than none at all.'

This is not a military history but the study of a rare personality, and does not seek to go over again the ground Field Marshal Slim covered in his monumental *Defeat into Victory*[3] but I should like to express my thanks to MacMillan and Company Limited, for permission to quote from that book. I am grateful to Field Marshal Lord Carver for permission to quote from two passages in his book, *Out of Step*, (Hutchinson 1989), and to Marshal of the Royal Air Force Sir Dermot Boyle, for permission to reprint an extract from his privately printed memoirs *My Life*. I should also like to record my particular indebtedness to the late Lieutenant Colonel Geoffrey Foster, A.D.M.S. to the 36th Division, who in his privately printed *36th Division: The Campaign in North Burma 1944-45*, recorded in detail the heroic campaign in which Festing's men defeated the Japanese in conditions and on terrain which the Japanese soldier had hitherto been thought to be invincible. His book is an invaluable source for information not otherwise

2. Later, Lieutenant General Sir John Cowley
3. Cassell and Company Ltd 1956

available. I am grateful to Penguin Books Ltd for the two extracts from K. C. Gandar Dower's *Into Madagascar*, published in 1943. And to the Ministry of Defence my thanks are due for permission to reproduce photographs of the war in Burma and elsewhere, taken by Army Photographic Units.

This book could not have been written without access to the Festing family papers and to the Field Marshal's personal records for which access I am grateful. I have been fortunate in being able to talk to and correspond with people close to the Field Marshal at various stages in his career — notably Major John Riddell O.B.E., his brother-in-law who was his ADC from 1943-1945, Brigadier John Cornell C.B.E. and Major Paul Greenwood who were his ADC's from 1954 to 1958, to Lieutenant Colonel Alistair Neilson M.B.E., his Military Assistant in FARELF, to Lieutenant-General Sir William Pike, K.C.B. C.B.E. D.S.O., his Chief of Staff in the Far East from 1956 to 1958 and to General Sir Cecil Blacker G.C.B. O.B.E. M.C. Military Assistant to Festing 1958-60, during his period as C.I.G.S. In addition to those who served with him in the Army I have also been fortunate in being able to talk to the Right Honourable James Ramsden, Under-Secretary at the War Office 1960-63 and Secretary of State for War 1963-64 and correspond with Sir Richard Way K.C.B., Permanent Under Secretary of State, War Office, 1960-63. But the judgments and mis-judgments, the mistakes and omissions are my own.

LYALL WILKES
Ogle, Northumberland

I

Origins and Early Days

The Festings, until the 18th century, lived in Schleswig-Holstein, and what appears to have precipitated the move to England was the death, in action at the Battle of Blenheim in 1704, of Captain Michael Christian Festin, ADC to Prince Eugene of Savoy. After the death of her husband the widow moved to England with her two sons under the protection of the Duke of Marlborough. The elder, Michael Christian (1680-1752), became the composer of over twenty concertos, Director of Music at Ranelagh, and founder of the Royal Society of Musicians in 1738, whilst the younger, John, a Doctor of Music, became 'eminent for his skill in playing upon the German flute and hautboy,'[4] a friend of Hogarth, and the subject of Hogarth's print "The Enraged Musician". When the elder brother died, Dr Charles Burney, whose denigration and jealousy of contemporary English musicians was notorious, wrote[5] 'with a feeble hand, little genius for composition, and but a shallow knowledge in counterpoint, by good sense, probity, prudent conduct, and a gentleman-like behaviour Festing acquired a weight and influence in his profession, at which hardly any musician of his class had ever arrived.'

Michael's son, a clergyman, was educated at Eton and

4. Works of Hogarth 1833 Vol. 1 page 63 edited by the Reverend John Trusler (Jones & Co.).
5. *General History of Music* by Dr Charles Burney (Volume iv).

Field Marshal Sir Francis Festing G.C.B., K.B.E., D.S.O.

Festing's Grandfather, Major-General Sir Francis Worgan Festing K.C.M.G., C.B.

Festing's Father, Brigadier-General Francis Leycester Festing C.B., C.M.G.

married Katherine Greene, daughter of Maurice Greene, Organist of St Paul's, Professor of Music at Cambridge and Master of the King's Music. Her portrait attributed to Allan Ramsay is still in the possession of the Festing family, whilst John's grandson, a Lieutenant-Colonel in the Grenadier Guards began the Festing association with that regiment. If it was the extraordinary military distinction and bravery of the Festings which was to become their outstanding characteristic, two brothers who each became Admirals in the nineteenth century, a Bishop of St Albans (1837-1907) and a Major General (1839-1902) who became Director of the Science Museum, then part of the Victoria and Albert Museum and an F.R.S., lent a variety of distinction to the family scene.

The Field Marshal's grandfather, Major General Sir Francis Worgan Festing (1833-1886) was wounded in the Ashanti war in 1873 and again in 1874 whilst trying to rescue a Royal Artillery officer who had fallen mortally wounded. For this he was recommended for the Victoria Cross and whilst this was not awarded, he was made in the same year C.B., and K.C.M.G. receiving the thanks of both houses of Parliament and became aide-de-camp to the Queen. Later he was awarded the Royal Humane Society's silver medal for rescuing people from a shipwreck, received the Legion of Honour for his deeds at the seige of Sebastopol, and became a nineteenth-century folk hero with public houses in Portsmouth and a street in Putney named after him to prove it.

The Field Marshal's father, Brigadier-General Francis Leycester Festing (1877-1948), married his cousin Charlotte Festing and they had only one child, the subject of this study.

The Brigadier-General had three brothers who all won D.S.O.s, and one of them, Major Harold England Festing of the Border Regiment, won the D.S.O. at Gallipolli, a Bar to the D.S.O. in France, four mentions in despatches and the *Croix de Guerre*. He died of war wounds in 1923. A brother-in-law, Arthur Hoskyns Festing C.M.G. (1870-1915) won the D.S.O. and five mentions in despatches and was awarded the medal of the Royal Humane Society for saving two African natives from drowning. He was killed in action at

Fromelles in France, leading a company attack. His bugler reported 'He was the bravest officer I have ever seen. He walked forward with a stick in one hand and a revolver in the other as if nothing was happening. . . .'

It was the Field Marshal's father who began the Festing military and social connection with Northumberland. He became an officer in the Northumberland Fusiliers but on reaching the rank of Major transferred in 1915 to the Royal Flying Corps. Severely wounded and appointed C.B. and C.M.G., he was later promoted to Brigadier-General.

☆ ☆ ☆

Frankie Festing was born in Dublin, where his father was serving, on 28th August 1902 and though from the outset the Army was to be his career, he did not go to the more conventional kind of school with a military background such as Wellington, but went, like his father before him, to Winchester. It never occurred to illustrious contemporary Wykehamists with whom he remained in contact such as the historian Charles Oman, or Roger Sherfield (later Lord Sherfield and warden of Winchester), that he was not their equal intellectually, and his interest in history was encouraged by the sophisticated ethos of the school. Festing was never an intellectual. He was that much more valuable commodity, a highly intelligent man. It was this combination of Winchester and Staff College, intellectual clarity with great physical courage, that was to make him such a formidable leader.

He did not much enjoy Winchester. His tastes were already too advanced for the usual team games to appeal and even then he was spending his pocket money on buying antique weapons and objets d'art. In marrying a first cousin in Charlotte Festing his father had taken a step against which geneticists might have cautioned, but Festing's extraordinary physical strength and stature and mental resilience showed how by great good fortune, his genes had taken the best characteristics from both sides of the Festing family and had given those characteristics an extraordinary intensity.

'We might,' said one of his sons happily, 'have all been

idiots — perhaps we are.'

Frankie was somewhat afraid of his father, a man of difficult moods and silences, but adored his mother who had a bubbling sense of humour, and she with her sister-in-law Eleanor (the Brigadier-General's sister) known as Aunt Nello, provided the two most profound influences of his early life. Aunt Nello lived for a great part of her life at St Jean de Luz in the Basque country. Increasingly with the years she wore the long black skirts and clothes of a French peasant woman and travelled everywhere on a bicycle with an engine of tiny horsepower attached to the front wheel. Since Frankie spent so much of the school holidays with her she provided him with a French tutor, and this was the source of his bi-lingual skill which was so much help to him especially in the later stages of his military career in the Far East and at Supreme Headquarters Allied Powers Europe (SHAPE) after the war. Aunt Nello had become a somewhat maverick Catholic convert and if one looks for the source of Festing's own youthful conversion one might not have to look very far beyond her influence. But more remarkably his mother, Charlotte, later became a Catholic, following in the steps of her son and Aunt Nello.

For a boy of sixteen from a Protestant family at a Protestant school to decide to become a convert to Catholicism, was only one sign of that independent spirit which sat uneasily with a reverence for tradition that was to dominate his life. His religion was going to be the real thing, not some new-fangled later edition. That such a man should eventually seek a bride from one of the most ancient of the Catholic recusant families of Northumberland — the Riddells of Swinburne Castle and Felton Park — was in keeping with a passion to make himself part of the mainstream of that Catholic tradition. Throughout his life he was punctilious in its observances. Woe betide the ADC, whatever the stresses of war, who could not tell him the nearest place and time where he could attend Mass.

Northumberland, whose devoted son by adoption Festing became, appealed particularly because of its links with a mysterious and distant Catholic past. The great Catholic families of Northumberland — the Widdringtons of Widdrington, the Radcliffes of Dilston, the Swinburnes of

Capheaton, the Charltons of Hesleyside, the Riddells and many others, living their intensely private lives and worshipping in their private chapels, fuelled an imagination left untouched by the more prosaic Protestantism of his Gloucestershire background, where the Brigadier-General and his wife eventually settled down in Hyde House, at Chalford.

The De Ridels were a Norman family who had fought with William at the Battle of Hastings and from 1314 had been Sheriffs of Northumberland, Constables of Norham Castle and later, merchant adventurers in Newcastle, being Sheriff and Mayor of that city many times. They left Newcastle in the seventeenth century to put a distance between themselves and the anti-Catholic mobs by buying the Swinburne Castle estate. The Riddells, unlike the Radcliffes, knew neither execution nor attaint, but Thomas Riddell of Swinburne was out in the 1715 rising and saved himself by escaping overseas from Lancaster Castle. He was later pardoned and allowed to return to his estate. Alienated from the spirit of the age and its political settlement, most of these old Catholic families lived on, quietly managing their estates, until the ninteenth century put an end to their disabilities and disqualifications from public office.

Festing's years as a young Rifle Brigade officer were probably the happiest years of his life — fencing, hunting, point-to-pointing, learning his trade as a soldier and, above all, ocean cruising in small sailing yachts. The Rifle Brigade Yearly Chronicles variously give his address as at Boodles Club, St James' Street, London, or at his family home, Hyde House, Gloucestershire, and the Chronicles carry several vividly written articles describing his adventures. In the 1929 Chronicle he describes how, with an unnamed Rifleman friend (who was in fact Godfrey Nicholson, later for many years a prominent Member of Parliament), he went for a month's jaunt in the Balkans, travelling third class by rail on seats so hard that Nicholson still remembers them, at a total cost of under £5 for the rail journey, travelling through Bessarabia and Roumania and coming within sight of Odessa.

Festing writes how mine host at one inn offered his

distinguished guests walnuts, cracking them between his teeth before graciously handing them round.

On the Liman estuary, opposite Odessa, Festing wrote — 'We were invited on board the so-called flagship (of the flotilla) whose captain, we were told, was a most accomplished scholar. Immediately after being introduced, he proceeded to address us in a language which was vaguely familiar, but it was not till he had been speaking for a minute or two that we recognised his oration as "Gray's Elegy". He afterwards informed us in French that this tour-de-force was the sum total of his knowledge of English. 'We were also struck,' he wrote, 'by the enormous number of rouged and powdered men, who may be seen parading up and down between the hours of six and seven in the evening, when the world of fashion takes its daily exercise.'

Always eager for new experiences, Festing had been granted three months leave in 1932 to become one of a crew of seven sailing a forty-ton yacht, the "Jolie Brise", across the Atlantic for the 1932 Bermuda race. That voyage took forty-two days averaging 141 nautical miles a day. His passion for the sea and sea-going yacht racing was to last all his life.

He found it difficult to overstate the importance to him of the two and a half years he spent as ADC to Major-General Sir John Burnett-Stuart (another Rifleman) when he was in command of the 3rd Division stationed on Salisbury Plain. During this time he could listen to Major-General Fuller theorising on the revolutionary role of the tank. Fuller's theories on strategy generally, and on the tank in particular, were more readily taken up by the German army than by the British. The Chief of Staff was that great man Archie Wavell. Festing wrote of this period, 'The ADC it is true was only a sort of appendage to the General, but providing he kept his ears open and his mouth shut he could not help but become increasingly sophisticated in military matters.' Sir John Burnett-Stuart wrote of Festing,[6] 'As for my ADC, I never had any use for the exotic type; I needed a good

---

6. I am indebted to Lieutenant-General Sir Norman Arthur K.C.B., Sir John Burnett-Stuart's grandson, for permission to quote this comment on Festing from his grandfather's unpublished memoir.

soldier (preferably a Rifleman!), an intelligent companion to go about with, and someone solid enough to put up with my tantrums; and in Frankie Festing I had all three. Incidentally, he was so large that I could always find him in any assemblage when I wanted him.'

In 1934 he signed on at a shilling a month on a Finnish three-masted iron barque of 900 tons, built in 1878, with a crew of eight men before the mast, plus boatswain, sailmaker, carpenter, steward-cook and mess boy to sail to Elsinore. He found "Oaklands" in Regent's Canal Dock, her masts towering above the tramp steamers looking, he wrote[7], 'like a thoroughbred amongst a lot of carthorses'. He described his spell at the wheel, 'It is great fun steering a big sailing ship and it was surprising how easily she answered her helm.' At Elsinore he finished up in the "Casanova" dancehall — 'a truly traditional ending to a voyage under sail, which is an experience that will soon be impossible to repeat.'

In November 1936 he arranged to visit Germany to stay with the Adjutant of the Second Battalion 82nd Infantry stationed at Gottingen and reported. 'The general life of an infantry battalion was extraordinarily like our own units. The men looked good material although I was encouraged to notice there seemed to be quite as many sloppy and dirty soldiers as with us. I had the impression that the presence of a foreign officer was an especial embarrassment.'

It was on this 1936 visit to Germany that he met a young German in the 82nd Infantry Regiment, Lieutenant Freiherr von Freyburg, with whom a strong mutual friendship developed. Freyburg was one of the guests at his wedding at Swinburne in 1937 and their friendship lasted until Festing was saddened by the news of his death in action on the Russian front in 1942. Festing was much helped to avoid the moral morass of a belief in collective guilt by the discipline of his strongly held religious view as to the uniqueness of every individual as a divine creation. He did more than anyone else, except Field Marshal Slim, to defeat the Japanese in Burma and much detested the

---

7. The Rifle Brigade Chronical for 1934 at page 202. The further issues of the Chronical give a good idea of the variety of Festing's interests.

Swinburne Castle, Northumberland, The Home of the Riddells

Festing at his marriage to Mary Cecilia Riddell

cruelty they had committed there, but again regarded these as crimes of the individuals who had committed them rather than as crimes of a whole nation. He had many Japanese friends and to the end of his days corresponded happily with them mostly on questions of Japanese Art and Weaponry. His was a singularly free spirit.

In 1936 Festing had gone through a period of uncharacteristic frustration at the slowness of his promotion prospects. He had always enjoyed his soldiering and was still enjoying it, but the knowledge that after sixteen years he was still in seniority only the tenth subaltern in the regiment, was sufficiently depressing for him to consider leaving the Rifle Brigade for the Gloucestershire Regiment where accelerated promotion prospects would have been on offer to him. He pursued his dissatisfaction in correspondence with the Military Secretary at the War Office. Thoughts of marriage undoubtedly helped him to feel unsettled at his lack of progress.

And so on 29th September 1937, in the private chapel at Swinburne, Festing married Mary Cecilia Riddell, elder daughter of Cuthbert David Gifford and the late Molly Riddell of Swinburne Castle and niece of Brigadier-General Sir Edward Riddell, a triple D.S.O. with five Mentions in Despatches. Festing, by this time, was thirty-five years of age, had been a subaltern in the Rifle Brigade for sixteen years and was still only a temporary Captain, although he had passed through Staff College with the highest grading the previous year. Promotion in peacetime was painfully slow especially for a good regimental officer who stayed with his battalion. For officers who were not up to battalion standard and left, promotion could be quicker, on the old army basis that if you wanted to get rid of someone, the best way was to promote him out. Festing had been commissioned into the Rifle Brigade in 1921 at the age of nineteen. In the thirties such slowness in promotion was not unusual even for an officer regarded as so highly promising as Festing. (There was in the Wiltshire Regiment a legendary Lieutenant Ludford who was reputed to have been a subaltern for twenty-six years!)

But Festing held on, hesitating to leave his beloved Rifle Brigade and his patience was rewarded with promotion to

Brevet Major in 1938 and in 1939 appointment to the Staff College as a Lieutenant-Colonel Instructor. General Sir John Cowley wrote, 'It was clear to his students that he was a man who took a broad view and was not interested in unnecessary detail — a man who would make his name as a commander rather than a staff officer',[8] a man who possessed that mysterious quality called leadership, so difficult to describe or to define, but so instantly recognisable when it appears.

But the war came in that same year and it was left to the Army, the scientists, the Navy, and the Air Force pilots to pick up the pieces left by the years of drift and disastrous foreign policy and to salvage survival. The intellectuals of the Left who had opposed the policy of appeasing Hitler very rarely did anything as sensible as joining the Territorial Army and managed to combine calls for military action with calls for disarmament and a contempt for the military virtues. Caught between the Chamberlainism of the Conservative Party and the intellectual frivolity of the Left, the armed services and the nation would have a perilous time of it.

---

8. D.N.B. 1971-80, page 312

2

Disaster in Norway, Victory in Madagascar

At the outbreak of war Festing was somewhat surprisingly recalled to the War Office where he was to remain reluctantly for a full year apart from three ill-starred weeks in Norway in April-May 1940. He had always been concerned with the problems of the flexibility of command between the R.A.F. and Army. The Fleet Air Arm was under Naval command — how could the R.A.F. act as the Army's artillery unless its bombers were under Army Command acting in direct and close support of the troops? These vexed questions gave rise to a dispute over command between Army and Air Force and to find the answer to these problems two new sections were set up, one in the Air Ministry and the other in the War Office, and Festing found himself as G.S.O.1 in charge of the War Office Section, with a Wing Commander as his G2. The Air Ministry section was headed by a senior airman with an Army G2 under him.

Festing confessed in December 1939 to feeling rather appalled at what had to be decided at such a late stage and not enamoured by what he called "The Siamese Twin Principle", adopted for tackling it. In the event, Hitler struck with his Panzer divisions before the solutions to these problems could be put into practice and complaints were many by the British Expeditionary Force in France at the lack of air cover which had been provided: but complaints turned to admiration for the victories achieved by the Air

Force against the Heinkels and the Messerschmitts when the battle was confined to the air alone.

His study of the most efficient joint use of land and air forces was to bear fruit in Burma but on the first morning of the war Festing had written, 'I was conscious of an immense gratitude to the Army for having allowed me such a wonderfully varied life, and I also had a great desire to escape the confines of the War Office and return to regimental soldiering.'

In April-May 1940 he had three disastrous weeks as a Lieutenant-Colonel (G.S.O.1 Liaison) at HQ North West Expeditionary Force (Norway), his only good fortune being to escape unhurt when his plane crashed in Orkney.

He had the frightening experience in Norway in the raid on Trondheim, as liaison officer to General Sir Bernard Paget, of what it was like to operate on foreign soil unbelievably without any air cover at all, against the vertical dive bombing of the German Stuka planes.

He had sailed in the cruiser *Manchester* for the fishing village of Molde, near Trondheim, but once ashore the party found it impossible to move without air cover. General Paget came to the conclusion that unless air cover could be provided, the expedition would have to be abandoned and briefed Festing to take that message to Lord Ironside, the C.I.G.S. Without a landing strip available he could not return by air. The village of Molde had by this time been totally destroyed by German planes and so he had to return with his melancholy message on the destroyer *HMS Arrow* which, to complete the tale of misfortune, was rammed by a Q ship disguised as a Dutch trawler and limped home to Scapa with a large hole in her side.

Festing wrote 'I went back to London and to my staff work as the Norwegian campaign drew to its unhappy climax.'

At the time of Dunkirk, although to his regret not in France, he was in charge of MO7, the Branch which handled air co-operation with the B.E.F., after the R.A.F. had been evacuated from France. It is difficult to feel that in this first phase of the war the best use was being made of Festing's abilities.

In September 1940, thanks to a chance meeting by the

roadside with Brigadier Oliver Leese whose car had broken down, and to whom Festing confided his wish to return to regimental life, Leese asked the War Office to release Festing to take command of the Second Battalion East Lancashire Regiment in his Brigade. This was, said Festing, "a magical transformation". He was thirty-eight years of age and this was his first command. He spent the next year in routine coastal defence duties in Sussex, alternating with rigorous training to bring his men to a peak of physical condition whilst fulfilling a counter attack role based on Horsham.

He was a successful and popular Commanding Officer and this was recognised in October 1941 by promotion to Brigadier in command of the 29th Independent Brigade Group, (which included the Second Battalion East Lancashire Regiment), with two future Generals, West and Stockwell, as two of his four C.Os. The Brigade went into intensive commando-like training in Scotland for several months, rehearsing assault craft landings, development and exploitation of a beach-head, and finally the rapid advance inland. Festing was the driving force behind this new type of training. The Brigade varied intensive training in the hills of Scotland with forced marches and exercises with landing craft from the Orkneys to just south of Inverary. Such was the high level of intensive training achieved that "showpiece" demonstrations of assault landings took place during 1941 before King George and Winston Churchill in Scotland.

The Brigade left Glasgow in a large convoy on 23rd March 1942, it was thought at first for new exercise beaches. Some of the troops had been issued with Arctic clothing as a security device to disguise their true destination, and duing the six or seven weeks voyage out it was also put about that Rangoon was the objective. It was a pleasant surprise for the Brigade when they reached hospitable Durban for a welcome five days ashore.

"We were part of one of the largest convoys to leave England during the war and we never learned what devious course may have been followed to bring us safely to South Africa — nothing to see about us but the other ships of the convoy, the sparkling sea, the flying fish, and at dusk the phosphorous jumping from the bows."[9] Two days out from Durban their objective was revealed — to take the 1000-mile long and 300-mile wide island of Madagascar, (the third largest island in the world with a population of three million), from the Vichy French to prevent the Japanese using the naval harbour of Diego Suarez for refuelling their submarines in order to attack our convoys coming round the Cape, and to prevent them attacking allied shipping along the East African coast.

For Festing who, as usual, had done his homework on Madagascar and on things generally, there were some distinctly ironic aspects of this expedition. General de Gaulle was to explode in anger at the news on 5th May 1942 that an attack had been launched by the British against French territory without a single representative of the Free French in the invading force. The lessons of Dakar had been learnt — namely that the Vichy French fought harder against other Frenchmen than anyone else. Secondly, because this was not, and could not be, an attempt to occupy the vastness of Madagascar but only to neutralise it and deny its use to the enemy, Festing and General Sturges knew they would have to rely heavily on the Vichy administrators of the island and keep the Tricolour flying from every provincial town hall, providing it did not interfere with militay operations or endanger security; indeed the Admiralty and War Office issued statements saying they had no intention of interfering with the French status of the territory which would remain French. Thirdly, (and perhaps most ironically of all), the British Government by this expedition was tearing up the Anglo-French Treaty of 1890 whereby it had been agreed that France would have a free hand in Madagascar in exchange for her non-interference with British plans in Africa. The result of that treaty had been the inevitable annexation of the island by the French in 1896 and the banishment of the last of the Malgache Royal Dynasty of the Hovas, Queen Ranavalona III, who had been well disposed to Britain and her missionaries, was a protegé of Queen Victoria, and had always been a thorn in the side of the French.

9. *The Blood-Red Island* by Rupert Croft-Cooke (Staples Press Ltd. 1953)

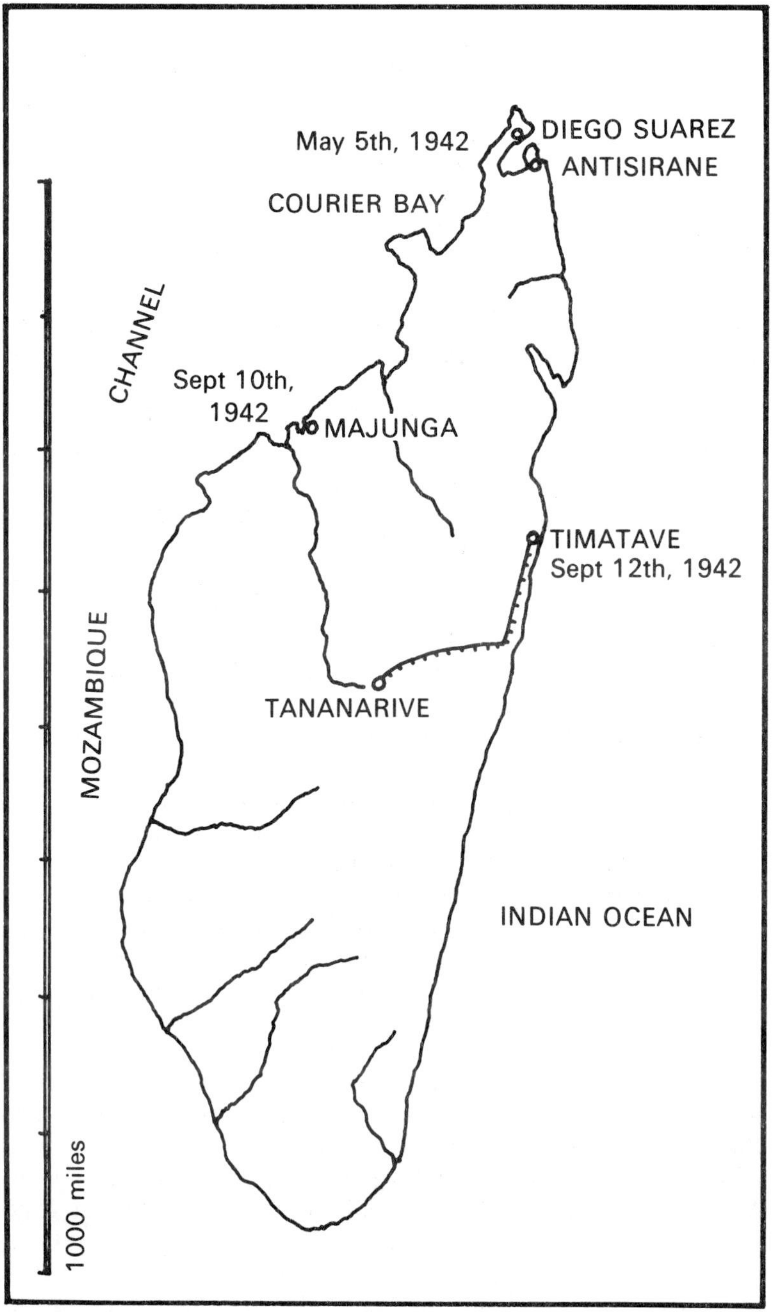

A map of Madagascar with dates of landings until capitulation 23rd September 1942

The convoy, with the protection of the Royal Navy under the command of Rear Admiral Syfret, with Major General Sturges, Royal Marines, in overall command and with Festing as military assault commander in charge of the beach landings, anchored off Courier Bay on the night of 4-5th May just out of range of the French battery. The immediate task was to capture the town of Antsirane and the naval base of Diego Suarez. The beach at Courier Bay was to be the target of four landing parties. *HMS Devonshire* was to silence the French battery if it opened fire. The landings, in a temperature of over 100° in the shade, were all successful and the beaches secured, but there was strong resistance around Antsirane and five of the Brigade's tanks were destroyed by French anti-tank guns. There was much sniping and vicious fighting with the Royal Scots Fusiliers in the thick of it. In two days the Brigade suffered over 500 casualties with 80 killed.

On the night of 6th May the night attack over-ran the French defensive positions and the East Lancashire Regiment within 29th Brigade occupied Antsirane. On 7th May Diego Suarez was successfully occupied. The months of intensive training had achieved its object. On this day a telegram was received from Churchill:-

> "Prime Minister congratulates you cordially upon swift and resolute way in which difficult and hazardous operation was carried through.
>
> He sends all ranks his best wishes and says that their exploit has been of real assistance to Britain and the United Nations. He was sure when he saw you at Inverary nine months ago that the 29th Brigade would make its mark."

Festing had been in his element organising the training for over a year which had brought his East Lancashire Battalion and his brigade to the physical and tactical peak which had so impressed Churchill. It was in the attack on Madagascar that Festing won his nickname of "Front Line Frankie" from the men of his own Brigade. He had been one of the first ashore to put into practice his great principle of always "leading from the front." Festing's D.S.O. citation said it all — 'continually in the more forward areas, carrying out personal reconnaisances regardless of danger and cheering up the troops . . . his leadership was always an inspiration.'

Rupert Croft-Cooke, then a sergeant in the Field Security Section, described[10] his role in the invasion after he had waded ashore carrying his motorcycle through the water at waist height.

'On the beach, the organisation was admirable — keep somewhere around the Brigadier's bren carrier, I had been told — a comfortable enough assignment one would have thought. A Brigadier, I argued reassuringly, would keep plenty of his forces in front of him — but I had not reckoned with Festing, our tall ginger-haired Brigadier. When the first shots were fired by the Vichy defenders of Diego-Suarez, hastily taking up their positions, Festing's bren carrier was several hundred yards ahead of the Brigade and the first casualty of the day was his driver who was hit in the hand. I saw Festing — alight and with members of his staff take cover among the roadside trees — just then I heard a tank, one of our Valentines, rattling up — at the same time Festing appeared from some bushes on my right — he looked unnaturally tall, I thought, an easy target for the enemy. He carried then, as always, a stick nearly as long as himself which suggested a shepherd's crook. He saw me and stood for a moment behind my tree.'

> 'Been fired on much, sergeant?'
>
> 'No Sir, not at all.'
>
> 'I've got to speak to that tank,' he observed with rather hurried chattiness.
>
> 'It's so hard to make them hear.'
>
> He strode across to the Valentine and started to bang on the turret with his long stick — it seemed as good a moment as any for me, so I got on my cycle, which luckily started with the first kick, returned along the road and rejoined my section.
>
> '— brigadiers,' I said profanely, 'who get themselves into the fighting.'

---

10. *The Blood-Red Island* by Rupert Croft-Cooke (Staples Press Ltd 1953) pages 25-26.

They were still nine miles from Diego-Suarez.

☆ ☆ ☆

After the capture of Diego-Suarez, Festing's men remained for five long months in occupation of the northern tip of the island, a peninsular not more than a hundred miles long and seventy miles wide at its greatest extent, before they made a move to capture Port Majunga on the west coast of the island on 10th September 1942. The reason for this long uncharacteristic delay is not known but it cannot have been any more welcome to Festing than it was to his Brigade as a whole.

It was particularly galling that whilst Festing's men were stationed in their northern base, the reason for their presence on the island — the Japanese naval threat — took the initiative and succeeded in sending into Diego-Suarez harbour at night a two-man submarine which blew up a large tanker and holing *HMS Ramillies*. The capture of the two Japanese in the submarine was scarcely compensation.

At the beginning of September, Festing's force embarked for Mombasa in the *Empire Pride* staying there for ten days, returning with Five Commando and an East African Regiment to Majunga, a town on the west coast of Madagascar which was their target. The brigade landed on the beaches on 10th September and surprise was almost total, but the fighting, by the time the town was reached, was real enough, with a dozen casualties in the brigade and bodies lying in the streets of the town to prove it. But except for the bitter fighting around Diego-Suarez there was an element of something formal and symbolic of "going through the motions" in the fighting, of men trying to preserve their future with Vichy if, contrary to their expectations, Vichy eventually were to win the war, just as the administrative officials welcomed any sufficient show of force which they were willing enough to accede to, but would never agree voluntarily to submit without it, since that would have cost them their pensions. Fighting for Majunga was over within an hour of the town being reached. The prisoners taken at Diego-Suarez, Majunga,

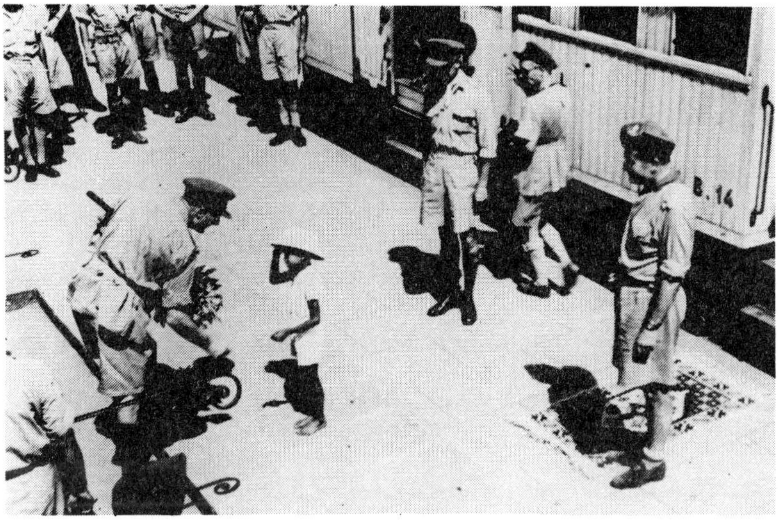

Festing receives a bouquet at Brickaville in Madagascar

and elsewhere, were transported to Durban where most of them enrolled with General de Gaulle's Free French.

The East African Regiment was ordered to march south east to take the capital Tananarive, but the greater part of the brigade proceeded to take ship and sailed to the north passing close to Diego-Suarez to take the port of Tamatave on the east coast. This time Festing's landing was to be preceded by a naval bombardment of the town from a dozen naval vessels in support, if the Governor failed to show the white flag. The white flag did not appear, but after a light naval bombardment lasting only four minutes the white flag appeared and the town was won. The Navy was disappointed by the speed of the victory.

'It was,' they said, 'nothing at all, we hadn't even started.'

The East Africans took the capital Tananarive without serious opposition on 23rd September by which date all the key points and harbours on the island were under brigade control and the island unconditionally surrendered. K. C. Gandar Dower in his book, *Into Madagascar* (Penguin Books, 1943) wrote — 'It was a brilliant experiment in combined operations, that knitting of land, sea and air power. One day when the offensive against the Japanese gets really going, the lessons that have been learned in Diego-Suarez, Majunga and Tamatave will bear important fruit.'

I do not think that either Festing or his Brigade felt many regrets at leaving Madagascar whose mixed Polynesian, Arab, Creole, French, Chinese and Indian peoples had little in common with Africa save their geographical juxtaposition and where the heat, the great forests and the giant crocodiles seemed to enervate and depress the spirit. 'For the men,' Rupert Croft-Cooke wrote, 'it had been an ugly and bloody little battle and six monotonous months in a foul climate,' but under Festing's and General Sturges' leadership the fighting had been brought to a successful conclusion and the Japanese naval threat to the Cape frustrated.

3

From Bombay Into Burma

The 29th Brigade sailed for Durban from Tamatave on 18th October 1942 in the *Empire Pride*, arriving there on 24th October. Christmas was spent in Durban in a relaxed atmosphere and the brigade sailed for India on 8th January 1943 transported by the Eastern Fleet under Admiral Sir James Somerville to the neighbourhood of Bombay. In the meantime, Festing, whose reputation had been much enhanced by his leadership of the Brigade in Madagascar had at the end of 1942 been promoted Major General. This promotion to command of a division is the summit of every professional soldier's ambition. 'A division — is the smallest formation that is a complete orchestra of war and the largest in which every man can know you.'[11]

It is a promotion which has made and unmade many reputations and it was to make Festing's. Whilst gathering his new division together he was put in charge of a combined operations training centre at Bombay, 'where we trained,' he wrote, 'for a series of Churchillian, I was going to say, fantasies but the main thing about it was that we were able to do a lot of training in combined operations with the Eastern Fleet. The 29th Brigade had had more experience of combined operations than anybody else at that time in the British Army.'

One day whilst he was engaged in this Combined Operations training on the Indian Coast, he took a friend's

11. F. M. Slim *Defeat into Victory*, page 3.

dog for a walk along the beach, and to entertain it threw sticks into the sea. The dog returned from one of its forays, not with the stick Festing had thrown, but with a beautifully carved figure from a seventeenth-century crucifix. Festing never discovered how long it had been in the sea, or where it had come from, but kept it with him throughout the Burma campaign and always regarded it as a symbol of great good luck which had helped to protect him. It stands today on the desk of one of his sons.

Collecting the elements of his new division together, and continuing the Inverary type of commando training on the broad waters surrounding Bombay, he awaited instructions. His main difficulty was that apart from the nucleus of 29th Brigade he had to build up his new division from scratch, even "winning" and creating a field bakery unit from a group of Indians, "lost" to the Army in some administrative mix-up, who had been sitting on a railway station without food for two days until Festing found them and "adopted" them. For months Festing awaited the rebuke that would arrive when it was discovered where the Indians were. It never arrived and they remained with him for over two years until the 36th Division was disbanded.

In March 1943 he was ordered to take his new division to Arakan, North Burma, to operate as part of General Slim's 14th Army.

"The Arakan", wrote Festing, "was a singularly unpleasant part of the world to fight in," and operations such as the defence of what were popularly known as 'Boxes', isolated posts in the Arakan, were undertaken.

The operation in Arakan was under the Command of Lieutenant-General Christison of 15th Indian Corps. The Corps comprised the 5th, 7th and 26th Indian Divisions and the 81st West African Division, with the 25th Indian Division and the new 36th British Division in reserve.

Festing and his new division were to play a leading role in the recovery of Burma after one of the most decisive military defeats suffered by any British Army in the twentieth century. But to understand this it is necessary to go back to December 1941. In that month while Festing was training his 29th Brigade near Inverary, the Japanese invaded Burma from Siam and captured Tenasserim. In

February 1942 in another theatre, Singapore fell to the seemingly all-conquering Japanese. By 9th March 1942 Rangoon had fallen, and in the same month Akyab on the Arakan coast was abandoned by the British and the R.A.F. were driven from Burma by the air attack on Magwe airport. After that the 14th Army was without air support in Burma.

On 15th April 1942 General Slim ordered the blowing up of the Burma oilfield and refineries and the Chinese 200th Division under General Stilwell was cut off at Toungoo. General Slim's attempt to stabilise a defence line between Prome and Toungoo had failed. By 20th May the forced withdrawal from Burma over the Irrawaddy river was accomplished, and the long retreat to Ye-u and to the Chindwin river at Shwegyin was completed. In five months the 14th Army's British, Indian and Gurkha troops and the Chinese Divisions under the air protection of the American Volunteer Group's P40 Tomahawks under Colonel Chennault had all been driven out of Burma in a 900-mile retreat. 'I had been put', said General Slim[12] 'in the normal position of a British General at the start of a war, called upon to carry out a task impossible with the means provided.' In June 1942 he was ordered to Calcutta to take command of 15th Indian Corps, to learn and to impart to others the lessons of defeat, and to retrain and regroup an Army to retake Burma. He had plenty to think about.

☆ ☆ ☆

Burma had until 1937 been part of India. Perhaps that too recent separation, with the many other defence preoccupations of 1937-39, had not allowed any very clear conception of Burma's place in any defence scheme of things. Indeed, so far as one can judge, the Japanese attack on Burma through Siam seems not to have been expected at all. And even after it had occurred, the war in Burma until the end of 1943 came very low in the order of priority for supplies and troop reinforcements; for example, there should have been an R.A.F. Bomber squadron there but only the

12. *Defeat into Victory*, page 14.

men arrived in Burma, the aircraft being ordered to stay behind in Malaya.

'On 31st January 1942', wrote Slim, 'we had thirty-five operational aircraft and the Japanese had 150. In December 1941 the air forces in Burma were almost negligible.'

Almost as disastrous was the separation of the headquarters of the air force which in Calcutta were 500 miles apart by air and unconnected by land with army headquarters at Maymyo, near Mandalay. Confusion existed as to whether the priority was the defence of Calcutta or the campaign in Burma, a confusion never entirely resolved, and aggravated by this separation of administrative from operational control.

Further confusion in command and strategy was illustrated when in mid-March 1942 General Stilwell took over command of all Chinese forces in Burma and was simultaneously appointed Chief of Staff to the Chinese Generalissimo Chiang Kai-shek. In his first role Stilwell was responsible to General Alexander but in his second role he was not. On several occasions Chinese divisions refused to obey, or procrastinated, in carrying out Stilwell's orders.

But the defeat, General Slim decided, had even deeper roots — psychological as well as tactical. The 14th Army had to be reconstituted to regard the jungle as an ally, never unfriendly, a cover and a source of operational surprise to the enemy, never so impenetrable as to be deemed impassable and never impossible for tanks unless it was precipice or swamp. Much equipment had to be lightened or discarded for the sake of freer jungle movement, and whilst supply from the air was the key, troops had to be trained to live off the country as well. Horses and packmules had to supplement machine transport so that the army was not tied to the few roads, which made them vulnerable to attack and the Japanese roadblock; when the Japanese set up roadblocks they could then be surprised and outflanked from jungle or scrub, rather than be confined to the road itself — 'Mobility and survival became synonymous.'

Slim preached this philosophy of a leaner, lighter and more mobile force to his army — even to quite small groups of them throughout his army, behaving and talking, as he put it, rather more like a candidate for Parliament than a General talking to his troops. It was a new message — though some of it had come from Orde Wingate and his Chindits — and had to be proclaimed with fervour and conviction by all his officers. Those who could not do so were dismissed. Slim had no doubt that eventually the more intelligent and flexible British, Gurkha and Indian soldiers would be more than a match for the unimaginative Japanese in single combat, but first his officers had to instil a sense of superiority over an enemy who had established a fearsome reputation for cruelty, even using prisoners and wounded for bayonet practice.

The weapon Slim used was the hand-picked small patrol of his best men to engage the enemy by ambush and surprise only when numerical superiority was in their favour, avoiding all large contact. It was these small skirmishes that helped to establish psychological mastery over the enemy in jungle warfare with many small successful actions — the Gurkhas sometimes returning with the heads of the enemy dead.

Slim created a new kind of army that made an ally of the jungle. By 1943 the reorganisation and retraining was well under way, General Christison took over command of Fifteen Corps and Slim replaced General Giffard as Commander in Chief of Eastern Army under General Auchinleck, and Mountbatten became Supreme Commander South East Asia and Allied Command. It was at that stage that on 1st February 1944 Festing, having received orders to leave Calcutta in advance of his division, arrived at General Slim's HQ at Calcutta to be briefed on the role allotted to 36th Division in the coming offensive in the Bawli Bazaar area, and the planned attack on the Maungdaw-Buthidaung road and on the Japanese positions holding the tunnel forts.

This, the second Arakan offensive after the disastrous battle of 1943, was to last only from February to May 1944 but was to be the turning point of the whole Burma campaign. It started badly with the Japanese 55th Division under Lieutenant-General Hanaya successfully attacking the Taung Bazaar area to the rear of 7th Indian Division. Their intention — to destroy Fifteen Corps and to take Chittagong as the first step to the invasion of India and the much heralded "March on Delhi." Captured documents made it clear that so confident were the Japanese of success that they had allowed only ten days to cut the communications, isolate and destroy the British forces in Arakan. Festing and his 36th Division were ordered to take the place of General Lomax's 26th Division Army Reserve.

But the tide was turned. Lomax's 26th Division recaptured Taung Bazaar and Festing moved into the Bawli Bazaar area. The enemy failed to destroy General Messervy's 7th Division in the Administrative Box in bitter hand-to-hand fighting that left five-thousand Japanese dead out of seven thousand. But the dressing station was overrun, the surgeons, still operating, slaughtered, the wounded on stretchers bayoneted, the Indian orderlies made to carry the Japanese wounded back to their lines and then shot. Messervy's 7th Division counter-attacked. The West African 81st Division advanced down the Kaladan Valley threatening the Japanese rear and then, to quote Field Marshal Slim[13] 'From the north swept down on both sides of the ridge, the 26th and 36th Divisions. The hammer and the anvil met squarely and the Japanese between disintegrated — destroyed to the last man in a snarling, tearing, dog-fight that lasted days with no quarter given or expected — Buthidaung was taken on the 11th March — It was then the turn of the 36th British Division to attack the last enemy stronghold defending the Maungidaw-Buthidaung road, the tunnel fortress. This they did with élan and skill. The Japanese resisted and counter-attacked at every step — but Festing's men were not to be denied.'

Lieutenant-Colonel Ronald Hamilton G.S.O1 at HQ 33 Indian Corps, and formerly ADC to General Auchinleck in India, was attached to the 36th Division from 17th February to 22nd March 1944 when the Division was engaged in the Bawli Bazaar area and wrote[14] — 'I conceived the greatest admiration and affection for 36th Division. It is a first-class show and this is due to Frankie Festing. He is young to be a Major-General and he is extremely able. He had read a lot, has very wide interests, he

13. *Defeat into Victory,* pages 243-244.
14. *The Wykehamist* 26th October 1976.

A tunnel fort defended by the Japanese and taken by Festing's men

shoots, sails, likes travel and is very alive. He is full of interesting conversation which he conducts in an attractively racy manner. He is very much a leader, and not a driver and thus one works very hard for him.'

'On 3rd March we moved our HQ in a southerly direction down the road to Maunghnama and I had a grand all-day expedition with Frankie. We walked many miles in the jungle of the Mayu Range among the forward posts — We were doing a good deal of shelling — the going was really formidable — I was impressed to see how many chaps in the division Frankie knew by Christian names and how pleased the troops always were to see him.'

Festing with his gift for vivid description described the claustrophobia of fighting in dense jungle as like "fighting a war inside a haystack."

This second battle of Arakan was the first defeat inflicted on the Japanese by a British force. The myth of the superiority of the Japanese as jungle fighters was there destroyed. Although in terms of numbers there would be greater victories to come, this was the decisive point of the whole Burma campaign and Festing and his men had played an important role in it.

☆ ☆ ☆

For nearly three months Myitkyina, the HQ of the 18th Japanese Division, had been besieged by a Chindit Brigade under Brigadier Lentaigne, by Chinese Divisions under Stilwell and by American Marauders. Relations deteriorated between Stilwell and the Chindits (Wingate had been killed in an air crash in April 1944) and at the end of May Stilwell — who had refused to serve under General Giffard of 11th Army Group and insisted upon being directly responsible only to Mountbatten, got his way to the extent that it was ordered that the Chindits would remain in the area only until 36th Division, refitting at Shillong in Assam, would arrive in the area and be placed under Stilwell's command when the over-exhausted Chindits would be flown out. On 3rd August 1944 Myitkyina fell, Mizukami the Japanese commander committed suicide and General Slim arrived at Shillong to address the 36th Division down to the rank of Corporal and tell them what he expected of them. It was, said Lieutenant-Colonel Geoffrey Foster, A.D.M.S. to the 36th Division, who heard it, a talk they would never forget — "they will probably never hear its equal."

He explained that he had chosen 36th Division for the task ahead first, because of its outstanding performance in the Arakan battle, secondly, because of his complete confidence in General Festing, and thirdly, because in his view the division was best suited to expel the Japanese from North Burma and to restore British prestige so badly damaged by the 1942 and 1943 defeats. The division would be supplied mostly by air and by parachute drops, and would be under American command (General Stilwell) who in the words of Lieutenant-Colonel Foster[15] "his face like an ancient turtle's, irascible and prejudiced, but a man to follow." Colonel Lyons of the United States Army would be attached to Divisional Headquarters as liaison officer.

---

15. *36th Division: The Campaign in North Burma* by Lieutenant-Colonel Geoffrey Foster (privately published)

The task was to clear the railway corridor from Myitkyina to Katha, clear the road to Mandalay and re-take Rangoon. It involved a fighting trek of nearly 1000 miles through swamp, scrub and jungle and the crossing of rivers. In fact the two brigades of the Division, the 29th and 72nd, would get no further than the region of Kalaw before being pulled out and flown back to India, but even that represented a fighting trek of over 700-miles and although they did not then know it, would take ten months, until in May 1945 the 19th Division would take over. They would see 'longer continuous service in Burma than any other British formation.'

In July 1944 the 36th Division comprised 29th Brigade under the command of Brigadier Stockwell (later General Stockwell) and 72nd Brigade under Brigadier Aslett D.S.O., a former rugby captain of England. But the Division represented an international team effort skilfully held together by Festing. Not only was he directly under the command of General Stilwell, but his air supplies and his tactical air support was solely in the hands of the USA 10th Air Force under Major General Howard Davidson as were the twelve light liaison planes carrying stretchers for the evacuation of the wounded. The Engineering Company for the building of air landing strips and the bridges which eventually bridged the Irrawaddy and Shweli rivers were also American and worked to great effect with 10 Indian Bridging Platoon and 15 Indian Engineering Battalion. Attached to 36th Division were three Chinese Batteries of Artillery also under American command as was an American mobile surgical unit where major operations would be carried out only two and a half miles from the worst fighting.

In August 1944 when General Slim addressed the Division at Shillong, although Myitkyina had just fallen to the Chinese, the airport had for some time previously been in Chinese, Chindit and American hands, so that 72 Brigade led the way on to the airstrip in the pouring rain of an early monsoon which in no way mitigated the steamy temperature. It took three hours to wade the three miles from the landing strip to the railhead waist deep in mud, weighed down by their equipment. It was a chilling and

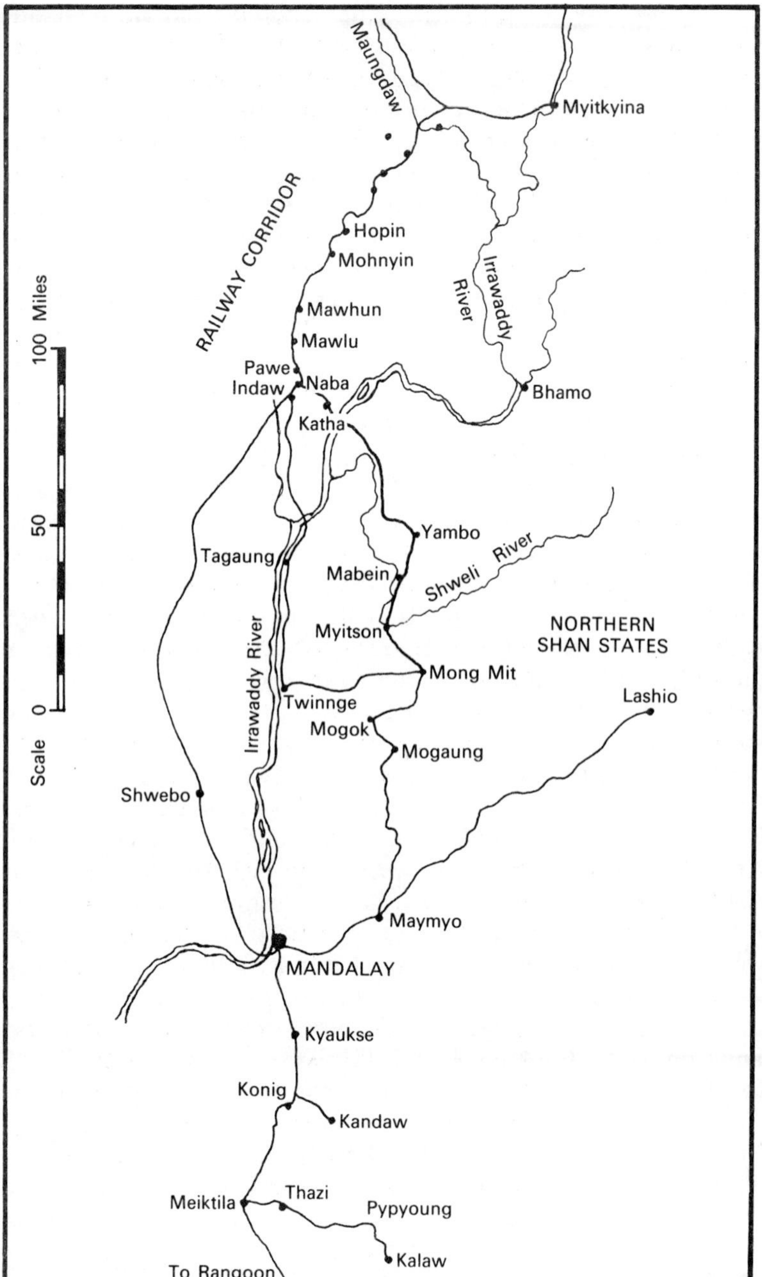

Map of North Burma and Arakan showing the railway corridor cleared by Festing's men through swamp, rivers and jungle, and the 1000-mile route to Mandalay

exhausting introduction to the kind of terrain over which the Division would have to fight along the 145-mile long railway corridor from Myitkyina to Katha which it was their task to clear. Having survived their introduction to jungle, swamp, snakes, leeches and Japanese snipers, 72nd Brigade began their trek to Mogaung some thirty-seven miles from Myitkyina crossing the river Mogaung on the way to Hill 60 ten miles south of Mogaung where it was expected the Japanese from their fortified positions would put up a strong resistance. They did, and a Reuter's report stated "the 36th Division, the first all-British unit to come under the command of General Joseph Stilwell, reported that 200 Japanese were killed in the first twelve days of the push from Mogaung. The unit fought in waist deep water and mud, the heat being intense between the rain."

The 145-mile long railway corridor had its road as well as its railway most of the way, but in places both were obliterated by neglect or enemy action and restoration proved a real test for the American and Indian Sappers. They also built thirty-two light aircraft strips and eight Dakota strips during the push to the South. Operating in these immensely difficult conditions the Sappers and the stretcher bearers took on a role as important as the infantry. As Lieutenant Colonel Foster wrote[16] 'A good stretcher bearer must be a man of good cheer, a philosopher: no miserable man could ever make a good bearer. During the watery months the qualities of these men were tested to the height of endurance — an army stretcher weighs about 30 pounds, the wounded man with his equipment at least 200 pounds, the bearer carries the same equipment as the infantry and in jungle warfare he must carry a weapon as well. Visualise the load, the country, the climate, the mud, the attention of snipers and the prevalence of ambushes, and consider the guts required to get the wounded in. I once watched bearers carrying a casualty up to their knees in thick mud, the two spare men assisting them to extricate their legs, taking over five hours to cover less than three and a half miles.'

16. *36th Division. The campaign in North Burma 1944-45 by Lt-Col Geoffrey Foster* page 15.

Men of the 36th Division crossing a Chaung

Festing was everywhere the work was hardest and the fighting fiercest, encouraging his men by Christian name and nickname, and always cheerful. It seemed that even in these appalling conditions he was enjoying himself

Major-General Festing in the Divisional Headquarters known as "White Horse Inn"

The railway line proved a blessing to the 36th Division for, in the absence of railway engines, the line was converted into a jeep railway (a jeep could usually pull three trucks on a railway line), all jeeps being fitted at the railhead with railway wheels to run on tracks. But the bridge over the Mogaung river had been badly damaged, and only partially repaired, so it could only bear the weight of one loaded jeep. What followed would have been a difficult operation in the best of circumstances; all the trucks had to be unloaded and all their equipment manhandled down to the ferry at the water's edge. They then had to be manhandled on to the ferry and manhandled off at the other side of the river. Finally, all the equipment had to be loaded on to the jeeps on the far bank with their road wheels now in place.

The Namsing Chaung, a small tributary of the Irrawaddy, proved less difficult, it being only thirty yards wide (a Chaung is any expanse of running water from a ditch to a small river). But a float strong enough to take one loaded jeep at a time was pulled across by means of a rope. All this meant difficult and slow progress and a fourteen- to fifteen-hour working day. Festing was everywhere where the work was hardest and the fighting fiercest, encouraging his men by Christian name and nickname and always cheerful. It really seemed that even in these appalling conditions he was enjoying himself. Certainly no Divisional Commander ever spent less time at his headquarters which was a railway coach previously used by the ousted Japanese commander and known to everyone in the division for some inconceivable reason as The White Horse Inn and as the division advanced, Divisional HQ advanced also, pulled by a jeep along the railway line.

He had the eerie experience in the railway corridor of being compelled to take cover from snipers, in a small burial ground in a clearing in the forest, and at the end of the engagement when he emerged from the shelter of the gravestone behind which he had been pinned down, found that the stone marked the grave of his own uncle killed in North Burma — 'Captain Worgan Richard Festing, 87th Royal Irish Fusiliers. B 1866, D 1897.'

Following the capture of Hill 60 the 72nd Brigade pressed

on and took Taungni, the enemy retreating to organise a stand further south. Taungni was chiefly noteworthy for the 200 Japanese corpses dumped in a bomb crater. Thaikwagon in heavily wooded country was captured by 72nd Brigade after severe fighting on 17th August. Festing decided it was now the turn of 29th Brigade to lead and they passed through 72nd at Thaikwagon and took up the chase to capture Pinbaw, twenty-six miles south-east of Mogaung, on 27th August. Festing received the following signal from Vinegar Joe — 'In getting your objective so promptly, congratulations to you and your men. Smart Work.'

The Japanese retreat slowed up at Mawlu. The brigade had covered thirty-six miles in fifteen days. All supplies that could possibly be dropped were being dropped by the American planes but some tail-end units were lagging behind and men of the 29th Brigade had be separated from their large packs for many weeks. Under Festing's close supervision everything not absolutely necessary was jettisoned to aid mobility. By this time the monsoon was subsiding in October-November and the Brigade had covered in all over 120 miles since July but despite Vinegar Joe's congratulations, Festing doubted whether they were going fast enough.

It was undoubtedly this impatience that led him to be up with his leading platoon and patrols cheerfully urging them on just before Mawlu fell on 31st October. When the Lieutenant leading the advance platoon was killed and the platoon Sergeant was about to take over, he saw that the platoon had a new leader — the General himself — surely the only Major-General in the history of the British army who has led a platoon to its objective under fire?

A conference had been arranged for senior divisional officers on this same 31st October at Mawhun for 5 p.m. By 8 p.m. there was no sign of the General. His unpunctuality was notorious — it usually meant (as here) that something more important had turned up. His sense of priorities was as sensible and flexible as his regard for military "spit and polish" was minimal — a man had to be clean and physically fit and that was all. By 10 p.m. his non-appearance, it was feared, could only mean the worst had happened. Who would now lead the division? "The General was dead, long live the General." At about 10.30 p.m. the lights of a jeep were seen bumping its way into the rendezvous area. The vast figure of the General levered himself out of the vehicle — 'so sorry if we have kept you waiting, but we have captured Mawlu — we have had a glorious afternoon, haven't we John?'[17] — this last question being addressed to his long-serving and long-suffering ADC Captain John Riddell.

Katha, at the end of the railway corridor, was now only thirty-one miles away and at the beginning of November, although the jungle was growing denser, the monsoon had almost come to an end and the weather was changing to a more kindly and temperate climate. It was in these circumstances that the Japanese made, at Pinwe, their last determined stand before the battle of Myitson on this section of the front, and at about this time Chiang Kai-shek at last got his way and Stilwell was reluctantly recalled by Mountbatten to be replaced by his deputy, General Sultan. Change was in the air and events were moving to a climax.

Around Pinwe in dense jungle, occupying heavily fortified positions, the Japanese fought with fanatical bravery in true Samurai and Bushido fashion and resisted all attempts of the 72nd Brigade to dislodge them. The thickness of the jungle prevented any flanking movement and the bitter necessity facing the brigade was for a frontal attack. Even though supported by a heavy air attack from the 10th U.S. Airforce with the brigade artillery and the Chinese gunners also laying down a barrage, little progress was made between 10th and 24th November, the Japanese refusing to give ground. Lieutenant-Colonel Foster tells the story of Lieutenant Kearns who 'fought a Japanese officer in single combat, rifle and bayonet versus Samurai sword. The Jap broke Lieutenant Kearn's right arm with his sword. The British officer fought on using his left arm and was subsequently wounded again on his right side. He killed the Jap officer and then died of his wounds.'

It was about this time that Festing added to his collection of Samurai swords by personally capturing two from

17. Lieutenant-Colonel Geoffrey Foster, one of the divisional officers waiting at the rendezvous, tells this story in his book in page 17.

The General does his own driving, sitting hunched up behind the wheel of his jeep, his driver is beside him

Japanese officers but the brigade's casualties were heavy, and Festing decided on 24th November to switch brigades and the 29th took over from the 72nd on the 26th November. The next day the 29th Brigade entered what was left of Pinwe only seventeen miles from Katha at the end of the 145-mile long railway corridor. In the 36th Division's advance the Japanese had lost over 1200 men with twenty taken prisoner.

After Pinwe, the Japanese were in further retreat and the division entered the villages of Naba and Indaw at the end of the railway corridor 200 miles from Mandalay, thus achieving their first objective in five months. In fact from Pinwe to Katha the enemy was scarcely seen at all, but the division was not to be allowed to spend any time in self-congratulation for the order was given that Mongmit, 100 miles to the south-east, was to be the division's next target, and it was hoped that Christmas dinner would be eaten there.

☆ ☆ ☆

Signs proclaiming the re-opening of the land route from Burma to China closed since May '42

To reach Myitson and Mongmit on the far side of the Irrawaddy and Shweli rivers, Festing decided to split the division, the 29th Brigade moving south of Indaw, crossing the mile-wide Irrawaddy river at Tigyaing and moving south upon Twinnge, approaching Myitson and Mongmit from the west, whilst the 72nd Brigade, reinforced by 26th Indian Brigade, would move south, crossing the river and approaching Myitson and Mongmit from the north, thus creating a pincer movement. Festing gave each unit a day off at Christmas, and eventually a Christmas dinner, from whole pigs to Christmas puddings, was dropped by parachute from American planes.

By early January 1945 the 29th Brigade, isolated from the rest of the division except from the air, took Mabein on 15th January, and Twinnge on 18th January. Brigadier Stockwell at this critical point was promoted to Major-General in command of an African division and left within hours, his deputy, Brigadier Bastin taking over. Brigadier Jennings commanding 26th Indian Brigade was ordered by Festing to pass through 72nd Brigade, take Myitson and cross the 300-yards-wide Shweli river. This attempt was made on 1st February but was beaten back.

Yet even more important than this temporary if bloody set-back was the fact that on 28th January 1945, the Chinese, British and American forces operating to the East of the 36th Division had reopened the land route from Burma to China, closed since May 1942. The reopening of this road from Ledo to China marked the beginning of the end of the Battle for Burma.

The attempt to cross the Shweli was made in American-designed Ranger rubber boats with outboard engines, each of varying size designed to carry five or ten men. The attempt on 1st February by 26th Indian Brigade to cross behind a smokescreen met with severe crossfire from light machine guns to mortars. Lieutenant Colonel Foster wrote, 'Seldom can the blooding of a formation have been so severe.' The brigade succeeded in establishing a bridge-head of some 80 to 100 yards — enabling 130 men to get across, but the bridge-head could not be enlarged and only five of the forty boats were undamaged. These had to be used to bring back what remained of the brave 130, '28 having been killed, 55 wounded, and 31 missing, leaving only 16 unscathed.'

The first attempt to cross having met with disaster, the next attempted by deception to mislead the enemy into thinking that an island in the river was to be the point of crossing. Obvious and much advertised preparations were made for this 'dummy' attack, a road was cut through the jungle opposite the island and "care was taken to allow at least one Japanese prisoner who had seen this, to escape." The enemy was fooled, and reinforcements were brought up to meet this spurious attack, whilst the genuine attack was made from the west at a point where tall elephant grass and jungle undergrowth provided cover just a little north of the junction of the Nammeik Chaung with the Shweli. Troops crossed the Nammeik Chaung unopposed whilst great "dummy" preparations drew fire on to the island. 'On 10th, 11th and 12th' wrote Lieutenant-Colonel Foster, our positions 'were shelled, mortared and attacked continuously day and night but the Indians not only held their ground but even managed to increase their hold. They were assisted in this by our own artillery and by the 10th American Air Force — it was evident that the enemy was straining every nerve to put paid to the division which had been pursuing him for so long.'

Field Marshal Slim describes[18] this battle as follows. 'Festing was pushing along his 36th Division. On the 9th February, in the face of determined resistance, he forced the crossing of the 500-yard Shweli river at Myitson, and with the help of most efficient American fighter and light bomber cover, held his bridgehead against all assaults including attacks by flame-throwers. After nearly a month of these attempts, and having suffered heavy casualties, the Japanese gave up the struggle and fell back south, contenting themselves with attempts to delay.'

But there had been several moments before this when the issue seemed to hang in the balance and at one point Festing crossed the river to confer with Brigadier Jennings as to the next move but the Indians held their ground breaking all attacks, and killing over 350 of the enemy. The importance of the Battle of Myitson, wrote Lieutenant Colonel Foster, 'cannot be overstressed — it meant almost total destruction of the Japanese fighting machine on our immediate front.'

With an immaculate sense of dramatic timing the Supremo, Admiral Mountbatten, chose the banks of the Shweli, opposite Myitson, to watch with Festing the American planes bombing the Japanese positions (see photograph at frontispiece). After the battle was over, to get the division across the Shweli a bridge was the only solution. In a great feat of field engineering the sappers and

18. *Defeat into Victory*, page 465.

Unveiling ceremony of the War Memorial to the 36th Division, Arakan, 1944

Mongmit puts on a brave show to welcome the 36th Division

Major-General Festing with Admiral Mountbatten the Supremo and Captain Riddell

The Mountbatten Bridge across the Shweli River, the longest wooden bridge built during the Second World War

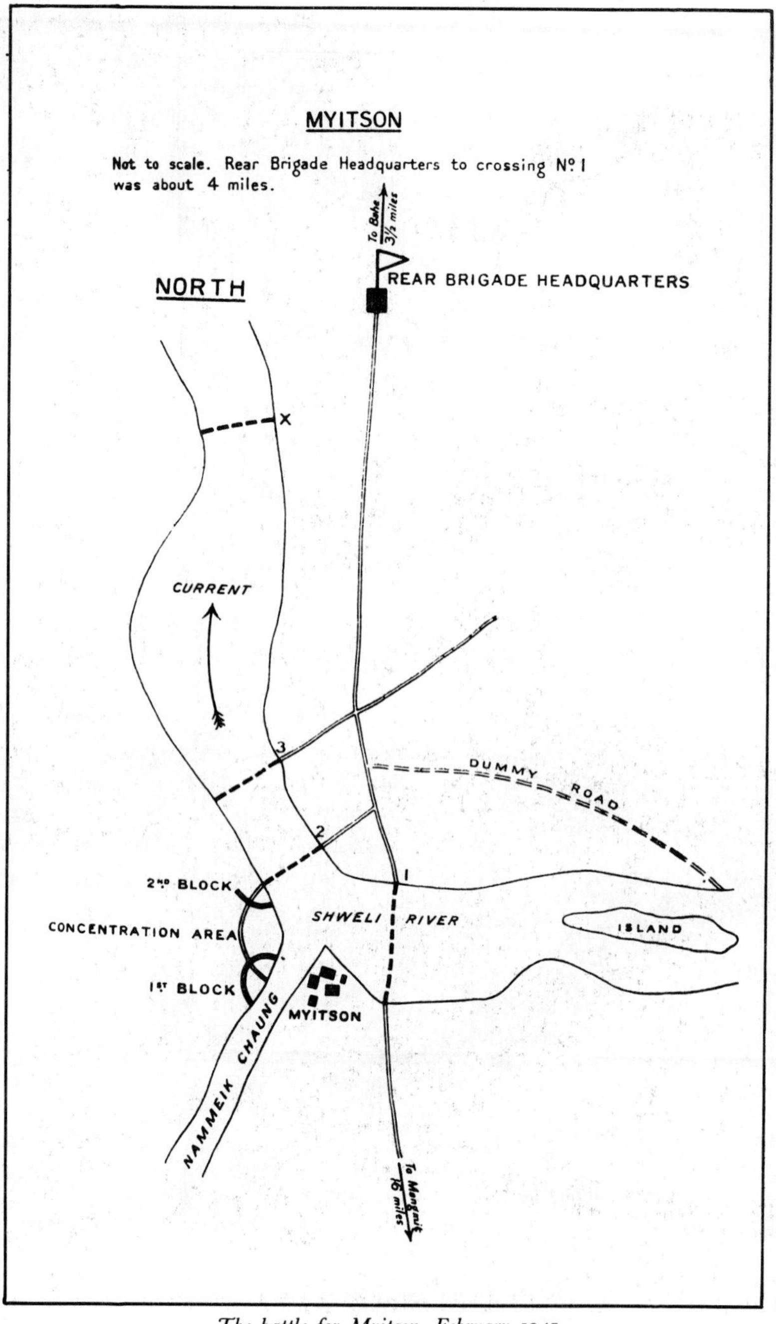

The battle for Myitson, February 1945

900 men of the 36th Division built the longest wooden bridge to be built during the war in nine days. With no power tools, using 950 Burmese teak trees with the island as the centre span. It was christened "The Mountbatten Bridge" (see photo at page 57).

Meanwhile, the 29th Brigade, having left Twinnge, and marched to the East joined up with 72nd Brigade at Mongmit. They had lost all contact with each other during the preceding three months. Mongmit with its temples and pagodas made a gracious contrast with the shambles that was Myitson where dead Japanese, piled high, made the stench and black flies insupportable. At Mongmit the 29th and 72nd Brigades after the most gruelling nine months, could even relax and listen to their commander delivering replies with great panache to the innumerable civic receptions and speeches of welcome delivered, of course, through interpreters. His innate affection for all Eastern peoples, including the Japanese, showed in the patience and courtesy with which he met the elders and civic dignitaries and sat through innumerable dinners and speeches with probably less sign of boredom than he would have shown at a Whitehall banquet.

Mongmit put on a brave face against the devastation of war. The ruler of Mongmit, the Sawbwa, was not only modern and pro-British, he had married an English wife. He and his family had been taken hostage by the Japanese on their evacuation of the area. The people of Mongmit were as pro-British as their ruling family and the elders, the local Buddhist priests and civic leaders, vied with each other in giving thanks to and praising Festing and his troops. A great garden party was held on the village green, gaily coloured umbrellas and canopies were unfurled[19] the bright colours adorning the women, the long saffron robes enveloping the priests and the soiled green battledress worn by officers and men made a strange contrast.

After tea, a rather lacklustre performance of national dancing by the women followed until, at a moment pre-arranged by Festing, the proceedings were brought to a discordant end by the wailing of the bagpipes of the 1st

19. *Lieutenant-Colonel Foster*, page 36.

Battalion Royal Scots Fusiliers.

And so on to Mogok, 190 miles from Mandalay, high in the hills of the Shan States with its ruby mines and sapphires, where General Sir Oliver Leese who had originally raised the 29th Brigade immediately after Dunkirk came to meet the division and talk to as many of the officers and men as possible. The division thought it was going to Mandalay but it was pulled out from Northern Combat Area Command on 1st April and had to say goodbye to its American friends. Field Marshal Slim wrote,[20] 'Festing and his division, besides a good fighting job, had done a great deal to dispel the cloud of uninformed criticism that at one time threatened to darken Anglo-American relations.' It was again an example of how Festing, undiplomatic in speech, dress and behaviour, by natural commonsense, lack of pomposity, and by consideration for others, achieved more respect and affection for things British than any smooth and more conventional approach could have done. He won the same affection from the Chinese attached to his division and this was to be a great help to him when, on the Japanese surrender in August 1945, he was flown from India to Hong Kong to be G.O.C. land forces in Hong Kong, with Rear Admiral Harcourt of *HMS Indomitable* as Commander-in-Chief.

Meanwhile, the division's objective was changed from Mandalay to more harassing of the enemy on the road to Kalaw, with new divisional headquarters established at Maymyo. But some elements of 36th Division were being airlifted to India for a rest from their arduous campaigning of the last ten months. Lieutenant-Colonel Foster wrote, 'It was more than an anti-climax. At the very last moment when part of the division was already leaving Burma, men were being killed and wounded in an endeavour to reach Kalaw.' But Kalaw was never reached before the division was evacuated — cholera, an early monsoon, and a temporary stiffening of Japanese resistance saw to that. By May 5th the division was held up all along the front. On 6th May 1945, 19th Division arrived and began to take over from the division. Two days previously, on 3rd May

20. *Defeat into Victory*, page 465.

HEADQUARTERS TENTH AIR FORCE
U. S. ARMY

A.P.O. 216,
21 March 1945.

Major General F. W. Festing,
Commanding, 36th Division,
Mongmit, Burma.

Dear General Festing:

For several months a substantial portion of the air-ground coordination bombing and air supply effort of this command has been carried on in conjunction with the 36th Division.

I desire to take this occasion to express my extreme pleasure in having had numerous opportunities to execute with your command operations against the enemy. The cooperation received by this headquarters and by units of the Tenth Air Force from all elements of your division has been truly exceptional in all particulars. All information desired concerning the disposition of the enemy's forces, the selection of bombing targets and the current ground situation was furnished us promptly and accurately. It is my belief that the joint air-ground operations carried out in combined fashion by the 36th Division and this command constitute an excellent example of coordination between arms and between Allies.

It has been my experience that Air Force personnel normally hold deep respect for the tough, hard fighting that is the lot of tactical ground troops. I believe that in this case such respect is far more profound than usual, as we realize fully under what difficulties of climate and terrain the 36th Division has been engaging the enemy. We deeply appreciate the display of confidence evinced by your command during our very close air strikes.

The truly outstanding accomplishments of your command in the North Burma campaign have been an inspiration to all Air Force troops operating in this area. May I express my sincere hope that we will have frequent opportunities to cooperate with you in future conflicts. I know that relations between all personnel of the 36th Division and the Tenth Air Force will continue most cordial in whatever joint duties we are assigned.

Most sincerely yours,

HOWARD C. DAVIDSON
Major General, USA
Commanding

1945, Fifteen Corps of the 14th Army had reoccupied Rangoon and the Burma campaign was over.

Festing accompanied the bulk of his division back to India by air. Had it not been for the dropping of the atom bomb and the Japanese surrender, the next job for Festing would have been to invade Malaya from the north, and he knew he had been earmarked as the Corps Commander. But as things turned out he was to be the only General in the British Army to have created a new division out of nothing and to lead it until it was disbanded.

When he returned to India he was awarded the Legion of Merit by the American Government and his ADC, Captain John Riddell, was awarded the Silver Star for gallantry in the action at Mawlu.

In 1956 when Field Marshal Sir William Slim published his book on the 14th Army and Burma, *Defeat into Victory*, he sent a copy to Festing inscribed — 'To Frankie Festing who did so much to put the "Victory" into the title of this book.'

4

General Officer Commanding Troops Hong Kong

The Japanese surrender in August 1945 raised new problems especially in Hong Kong even if it resolved some old ones. Relations with China in general, and with Chiang Kai-shek's nationalist armies and the Chinese communists in particular, posed difficult problems for the Allies and especially for Britain. There was a danger that in the euphoria of the Japanese defeat, with each Chinese faction jockeying for position and needing a propaganda victory to improve their post-war status, they — and Chiang Kai-shek in 1945 in particular — might not wait until Britain's future in Hong Kong was the subject of negotiation but would invade. Massive Chinese armies were poised on China's mainland within easy striking distance of Hong Kong.

During the war with Japan, Britain had agreed that Hong Kong should be included within Chiang Kai-shek's operational command area and when the surrender of Hong Kong was about to take place, the Generalissimo publicly announced that he had delegated the power to accept the surrender to the British. In this he over-reached himself, for such a purported delegation was a derogation of Britain's sovereignty over the Crown Colony and so, totally unacceptable to the British Government. Britain's moral and legal position was strong but in military terms was weak. As General Carton De Wiart wrote[21] — 'What the people of

21. See his *Happy Odyssey* at page 272 (Cape 1950).

England did not seem to realise was that if the war had continued for another few weeks, the Chinese would have taken Hong Kong from the Japs by themselves.' It was in these strained circumstances that Churchill and Mountbatten decided to send out Festing from India to be General Officer Commanding troops, Hong Kong.

General Carton De Wiart, who had been sent out by Churchill to be Chiang Kai-shek's special emissary wrote[22] 'British diplomacy may have been questionable at this time, but the choice of personnel was inspired, and the situation was saved by two men, Admiral Harcourt, who took the surrender and became the first post-war Governor of Hong Kong, and General Frankie Festing G.O.C. Troops, Hong Kong. These two men by their tact and integrity smoothed away every difficulty as it arose and what is more, prevented other difficulties arising. The Chinese held them both in affection and respect and it is to their credit almost alone that we owe avoidance of the most serious trouble.'

Mountbatten expressed a similar view later [23] of 'my old friend Festing' — who knows his stuff and is trusted and respected.'

His policy in Hong Kong was to express a loud disbelief to Chinese Army leaders that they would not be so foolish, for the sake of what might look like a short-term advantage, to sacrifice their own — and Hong Kong's — long term interests, at the same time building up such forces as he could to deter just such a mistake being made. By February 1946[24] 'over 65,000 Chinese troops had been through Hong Kong, and General Festing said the military in Hong Kong worked very closely with them. He said he personally knew many of the commanding officers and this proved a great help.'

Building up the Hong Kong garrison went with visits to China's army leaders in Chungking, Canton, and Shanghai and many soothing words were spoken. In Chungking he praised the fighting qualities of the Chinese soldier and his sense of humour. He was reported in the Press as saying

---

22. See his *Happy Odyssey* at page 272 (Cape 1950)
23. *Mountbatten*, by Philip Ziegler at pages 580 and 611 (Collins Ltd)
24. *The Chinese Morning Post* and *Hong Kong Telegraph*, 12 February 1946.

Major-General Festing with Rear Admiral Harcourt and Chinese Commanders in Canton, May 1946

'He was justified in paying this tribute because of his long association with the Chinese Army in Burma.' He was entertained to dinner by Chiang Kai-shek and the Commander in Chief of the Chinese Armies, General Chen Cheng. Referring to Hong Kong, the General said — 'There is a big field for co-operation between us down in Hong Kong and all of you in China. Hong Kong and Canton are inseparable, geographically they must be and sentimentally they must be.' In return, many Chinese leaders were entertained by Festing in Hong Kong including Mr T. V. Soong, the Generalissimo's brother-in-law. For a man of his large bulk he walked the diplomatic tightrope with a suprising delicacy and defused the danger of any imminent Chinese invasion. Indeed, in January 1946 in Canton he had been invested by the Chinese Government with the Order of The Cloud and Banner as a mark of their esteem.

He had now been on arduous active service since 1940 and it was doubtless a welcome, if somewhat surprising

Festing invested by Chinese Government with The Order of the Cloud and Banner, 1946

posting, when in 1946 he was posted to the War Office in London as Director of Weapons and Development and in the same year was appointed C.B.

5

The War Office and Return to Hong Kong

Such a posting must have been particularly welcome to Mary Festing who had given a gentle hint, by her purchase of a house in the North Tyne valley of Northumberland in 1944, that she would not look too kindly on continuing indefinitely after the war to live the itinerant life of a General's wife, but wished to have a permanent homelife in Northumberland with her sons. As to Festing himself, with a world ostensibly and intermittently at peace, it would become increasingly difficult to find a role for his particular talent for inspiring leadership. Templer would find such a role in Malaya but for the moment London claimed Festing, as it had not done since 1940.

He applied his unquenchable enthusiasm to the problems posed by weapon development and employed his gift for vivid speech to illustrate just how difficult the problems were (which is doubtless why so many of them are still unresolved to this day). In a lecture which he delivered on 11th September 1949, he said that as Director of Weapons, he had gained a completely new insight into the problems of designing new weapons.

'The War Office should state clearly what the weapon should be capable of doing but must not suggest how those needs must be met. This is the designer's field, and the designer must be given a completely free hand. The time needed is considerable so the Director must look ahead for at least ten years. In one case it took two and a half years and 274 modifications to get it right. For an anti-aircraft gun, nine and a half years were necessary. The costs are enormous. In 1949 the pilot model for a big tank cost about half a million pounds. Even a fifteen-hundredweight truck cost £250,000 to develop, for commercial trucks are no longer strong enough or powerful enough for war purposes. In 1939 the average tank weighed seven tons and would cost about £7,000 to produce. In 1949 its weight was 45-50 tons and cost £40,000. Machines take the place of men, and firepower increases with less and less manpower.'

But because he had always found commanding men infinitely preferable to being in charge of their machines, it was a welcome move when in June 1949 after two and half years as Director of Weapons and Development, he received his second summons to go to Hong Kong to be the General in charge of a unified command of all sea, land and air forces — at that time a command unique in peacetime.

The situation was no less difficult than it had been when he had been first ordered there in 1945 to take command of Hong Kong at the time of the Japanese surrender but by this time the threat to the colony came not from the nationalist forces of Chiang Kai-shek but from the victorious forces of Communist China. If General Carton de Wiart, who had been sent out by Churchill to China in 1945 as his special emissary, is correct in his assessment that the Chinese forces, had they acted, could have captured Hong Kong in a week, the Chinese forces now within reach of Hong Kong in 1949 were more numerous and determined even than before. The Labour Government and its Defence Minister, Mr A. V. Alexander, were concerned at the fragility of Hong Kong's defence position and the sending out of General Festing at such a time to take charge showed how high his reputation stood.

As always, Festing took the bold initiative, stressing in public speeches and at frequent Press conferences the daily increasing strength of Hong Kong and the reinforcements arriving. He was one of the first generals to realise the importance of "going public", taking the public into his confidence and at the same time warning off any potential enemy. What had been a 12,000 garrison strength would soon, he proclaimed, be 30,000 strong including 2,000 Royal Marines in No. 3 Commando Brigade, with two squadrons of Spitfires and a Royal Naval presence that guaranteed mastery of the sea, whereas, he recalled, when Hong Kong had fallen in 1941 the Japanese had been masters of the sea and air.

When he had finished a speech to the Press he always encouraged questions instead of treating them as a form of not-so-dumb insubordination. Asked if the colony could resist a sustained attack, he replied: 'I am completely confident that I can fulfil the function given to me by Mr Alexander.' When asked by a Chinese correspondent what would be the position if retreating Nationalist troops were to come over the border for refuge, the General replied with a smile, 'What we will do is something that I have got to work out for myself.'

He showed that two and a half years at a desk job in the War Office had not dulled his appreciation of the importance of leading by example or his zest for being out and about. Whether it was a new battalion arriving, or Lieutenant Commander Kerens of the *Amethyst* on the run after a shoot-out with Chinese communist forces on the Lower Yangtse, the General would always be there on the harbour steps to welcome and to direct and to warn.

'Although Hong Kong is a highly vulnerable target, it is in some ways relatively easy to defend. Fire will be very concentrated which means it can produce a very much higher gun density. The gun density of Hong Kong when complete would compare favourably with London during the height of the Blitz in the last war.'

He confessed his problems to the public: 'my biggest headache is the water supply problem as it was in 1941. This colony has never been sufficiently well conscious, but Army engineers have discovered and are discovering much more well water. The other problem is inflation but I am afraid I cannot do much about that. It is a particular problem for troops coming out here; there are wonderful things to do and see but not a wonderful supply of money to buy anything with.' He acknowledged, to the general population of the colony, the problems presented by directing into a confined area so many troops.

'Thirty-six new camps are being built, roads are being constructed in the colony for the first time with modern earth-moving machinery.' In addition to solving the water problem, Festing formed the new 40th Division under Major General G. C. Evans with a full regiment of anti-aircraft guns set in cement and steel foundations. The defence preparations for Hong Kong, said Festing 'were mostly hard work and bloody sweat' and all the time military training and exercises and sport had to keep his soldiers fit whilst encouraging their integration so far as possible with the civilian community around them.

It was as part of his campaign to forge links with the community at large that he delivered an address at the Catholic centre in which he gave a forceful and vivid account of some of the difficulties in building up a new force. *The China Mail*, on 1st September 1949, commented 'General Festing has not been in the colony very long apart from his term here during the immediate post-liberation period, but he already has a grasp of the situation second to none. So when he said yesterday that we can now be successfully defended against any attack, residents can breathe more freely than they have done for some time past.'

But for once his health proved he was only human. *The China Mail* of 13th September 1949 carried a valedictory editorial under the heading "A Serious Loss" which said it all. 'The news that General Festing is being flown back to England because of illness will come as a shock to many people in the colony. It is not conventional politeness but a plain statement of fact to say that his departure will be most deeply regretted by both troops and civilians. The tall, massively-built soldier with the disarming grin and the completely natural manner was the ideal man for the complex and difficult task he was brought out here to do. He has "a way with him," and his approach to people puts them at ease whether they be Ambassadors or National Servicemen. He had the unique task in peacetime of co-ordinating all the armed forces under one command — his own — and seldom has such a transition of authority taken place so smoothly. Competent observers, of whom there are a number in the colony, state the military organisation here is a model of efficiency.

In his relations with the public and the Press, the General

showed a keen sense of the psychological side of armed preparations. His was not the hidebound approach which considers that civilians should mind their own business while experts keep their own counsel on defence matters. He announced clearly what his intentions were, what the situation was, and by doing so won trust and respect. One can only hope for a successor who will share his views.'

Such was the impression he had made in only three months in the colony.

☆ ☆ ☆

It had never seemed very convincing that Festing would have relinquished his command and been flown home because of the sinus trouble given as the reason in the Press. In fact, he had a blood clot on the brain and nearly died. He was so ill that he was carried on a stretcher to his Dakota with a doctor and nurses in attendance. His plane was met at Heathrow by General Sir Gerald Templer, Vice-Chief of the Imperial General Staff, who wrote to Festing's mother: 'I do not wish to be alarmist but I am afraid Frankie is pretty ill. I judge this from the fact that I have had a telegram from General Sir John Harding in Singapore saying that Frankie had stayed the night in his home but that he, John, had not been allowed to see him. His wife, who is expecting the birth of her fourth child, writes to say she hopes he will get some leave when he is well since he has not had more than ten days since the beginning of the war. I have had a message from Buckingham Palace saying that a message of sympathy should be passed to Frankie on his arrival in this country from His Majesty the King.'

He was operated upon in the Radcliffe Infirmary in Oxford. Thanks to the skill of the surgeons, his own strength and will to recover (he was only forty-seven years of age), he did make a miraculously full recovery. But the recovery could only be tested by the passage of time, so stress and active service was out of the question for a while. He took several months' leave and in 1950 at a stage in his convalescence, was appointed President of the Regular Commissions Board. Although technically still an invalid, so important did he regard the correct choice of officers that he insisted on personally interviewing all the candidates — a task no predecessor had assumed.

This was the nearest he ever came to being a Whitehall Warrior and although he did not take kindly to the role the job gave him the time he needed to clarify his thoughts on the army he wanted for the future — a technically advanced volunteer professional force with the abolition of National Service. This was not to come about until December 1962, but from the early 1950s he was its strongest advocate. He recognised the great contribution that the National Servicemen had made in the recent past and the immense benefit it had conferred on the serving generation but the increasingly technical complexity of the weaponry made it increasingly impossible to run the army as one of the departments of social service — whatever its benefit to the national life might be in terms of physical fitness, literacy and discipline.

At a Burma Club dinner he said — 'National Service saved this country. The National Servicemen taught the army a good many things and we are grateful to them. Those who decry the young men of today are very foolish. But voluntary service is the only basis for an army to-day — well equipped, well trained, with a sense of purpose, highly mobile and requiring co-operation with the Navy which has to transport them with their equipment, and air mastery, was vital — an army trained to do its job anywhere it is needed, will encourage our friends, of whom we have quite a lot, and discourage our enemies of whom we also have a few.'

6

Eisenhower's Assistant Chief of Staff, Supreme Headquarters Europe and Egypt

In 1951 when it was clear he had made a complete recovery from his illness, he was appointed General Eisenhower's Assistant Chief of Staff (Organisation and Training), Supreme HQ Allied Powers in Europe (SHAPE). The HQ was at Marly, some twelve miles from Paris. His task was really a continuation, but on a much larger and on an international scale, of the weapon standardisation work he had begun in London as part of his duties as Director of Weapons and Development. The eight nations at SHAPE (Americans, Belgians, British, Dutch, Danish, French, Italians and Norwegians) worked for a uniformity and interchangeability of weapons which would simplify weapon and ammunitions production in peace and war. It was an attempt to teach that collective security began at the drawing board; an attempt to create an international team of military experts acting and thinking not as national representatives, but owing a wider loyalty to the Supreme Headquarters that was to herald the NATO organisation.

Even individualists such as Montgomery, responded to the efforts of Eisenhower and General Gruenther to build up a teamspirit amongst the eight member nations. Festing's gift for friendship ensured that he got on as well with his European colleagues as he had done with his Far Eastern ones and he became a popular figure at HQ. Indeed, the opinion has been expressed by members serving at HQ that, had Festing been in charge rather than Eisenhower, he might have been able to bring his personal charm and formidable powers of persuasion to bear to persuade de Gaulle not to take the French out of the organisation.

His efforts at SHAPE resulted in wider recognition of him as a man of commonsense who could be trusted. He was made K.B.E. in 1952, and, in April 1952, succeeded General Erskine, arriving in the Canal Zone as G.O.C. British Troops in Egypt where he was to remain until 1954. Mountbatten wrote him a congratulatory note from SHAPE Headquarters saying truthfully 'I well know how delighted you will be to be with troops again!'

The argument about British troops East of Suez was just beginning, but his immediate task was to maintain the safety of the lines of communication on which British shipping, supplies and security depended and in particular to maintain the safety of the Suez Canal. Like much of what he strove for, his efforts to maintain the Suez position were defeated by future events and by the Suez failure of 1956, just as his efforts to maintain British rights in Hong Kong would be negotiated away from 1997.

Asked whether he preferred working under a Labour or Conservative Government, Festing replied: 'Definitely under Labour — for under Labour the Minister of Defence will very likely be an ex-lance corporal who knows nothing, and knows he knows nothing, and will be prepared to accept military advice, whereas in a Conservative Government the Minister of Defence will probably be an ex-Major in some pretty ineffectual Yeomanry Regiment and thinks he knows it all.'

For a time Festing got on particularly well with Manny Shinwell, Labour's Minister of Defence until the 1951 election who had not even been a lance corporal and who had been gaoled in Glasgow for riotous conduct. This somewhat unlikely alliance between Festing and the tailor's cutter and ex-revolutionary from Glasgow became strained in July 1953 when an airman on leave in Ismailia was abducted from his hotel by Egyptians and disappeared. Festing, as General Officer Commanding British Troops in Egypt, announced that unless Aircraftman Rigden was returned unharmed within a time limit he would set up roadblocks at all entrances to and exits from the town for searches, and would prevent supplies and foodstuffs reaching the town.

In July 1953, during the Premiership of General Neguib, British troops were not infrequently murdered or abducted in the Canal Zone, and Festing's strong measures were supported in the House of Commons by the Minister of State, Mr Selwyn Lloyd: 'All that was said was that if the man was not returned by a certain time certain measures would have to be taken which would be inconvenient to the civilian population.' But Mr Shinwell in questions on 15th July wanted to know whether General Festing had consulted with the British Ambassador in Cairo before announcing these measures, Mr Wyatt wanted to know whether the General had communicated his intentions to the Foreign Office before his pronouncement, and Mr Noel Baker predictably asked whether it was not clear that the best way of avoiding such incidents in the future was to have new negotiations? By 27th July Mr Shinwell was huffing and puffing the other way: 'Is there to be no adequate protection afforded to members of Her Majesty's Forces in Egypt?'[25]

There are always a number of persuasive reasons for consulting rather than for acting and always a number of people only too anxious to limit the discretionary exercise of a commander's authority to safeguard the lives of his troops, but Festing was not a man who needed directions or guidance on such matters and in the end the airman was returned unharmed and for the immediate future, the number of such incidents in the Canal Zone declined.

☆ ☆ ☆

Festing's arrival had coincided with increased agitation in the Egyptian Press against the presence of British troops. The newspaper *El Musawa's* comments on 22nd January 1953 being fairly typical.

'The British are still clinging to their old ideas which

---

25. See Hansard 27th July 1953.

leads to occupation, the same ideas that prevailed 70 years ago. Listen to what Sir Francis Festing told us — The importance of the Canal today is the same as on the day it was inaugurated. Methods of war may have changed but the principles have not — We can excuse him. He is a soldier. For him victory goes to the strong. The strong know nothing of rights nor the rights of peoples — they take it for granted that their Zone is part of their Empire. Why will Britain not leave Egypt peacefully?'

Although relations between the British and Egyptian Governments became increasingly subject to strain between 1952 and 1954, ordinary Egyptian civilians remained outwardly friendly and courteous. Festing decided to concentrate on keeping his troops at a peak of physical fitness and presided over the biggest peace-time exercise in Egypt of over 20,000 troops which lasted several days. In May 1953 he attended the accession ceremony of King Hussein in Jordan and there resumed old acquaintance with Sir John Glubb, relaxed on duck shoots, acted as host to Queen Elizabeth's Coronation Party at Flagstaff House, Moascar, on 2nd June 1953, and entertained widely and well visitors from England of all political persuasions, ranging from Rifle Brigade Tory MPs such as Sir Charles Mott Radclyffe, to Mr and Mrs Aneurin Bevan.

His robust "no nonsense" approach both to the Egyptian authorities and to his own troops succeeded in preventing local conditions from deteriorating further in spite of the increasing tension between the Egyptian and the British Governments. In 1954 he was surprisingly recalled to the mundane job of G.O.C. Eastern Command when his famous interview with his Chief of Staff (later Lieutenant-General Sir John Cowley) took place at Hounslow as follows:-

'I do not like this part of England and I will be away for most of the time' (He was as good as his word). 'When I am away you make all the decisions without referring to me. When I return, if the War Office questions your decisions I will tell them that you are right and they are wrong — but I may not always tell you that and if you continue to make decisions that I consider wrong I will find another Chief of Staff.'

Aneurin Bevan and Jenny Lee visiting Lieutenant-General Festing in Egypt, 1953

7

General Officer Commanding Eastern Command and Commander in Chief Far East Land Forces (FARELF)

The gratitude he felt for the kindness shown to him by General Burnett-Stuart in early days was reflected in the way he treated his own ADCs in later years. Indeed, except during his time as C.I.G.S. when the flat provided was too small for this, Frankie's ADC lived with him at his home and was treated as a son. His general method of dealing with his staff was effective but not to everyone's liking. As a General he had a large staff but he would consult only with those whose judgement he trusted — usually his Chief of Staff, Military Assistant, and his ADC. With these he confided frankly while completely ignoring senior members of staff in whose judgement he had less confidence.

Fortunately, he was a good judge of whom to trust and whom not, and they rarely let him down, but those outside the charmed circle felt excluded and diminished. He never sought consensus. He believed there was a right and wrong solution to every problem and that there was always one overwhelming consideration pointing to the correct one. Every good lawyer knows this is true and he brought to his problems a legal precision of thought that was remarkable in a soldier.

He was fond of quoting from what had probably started life as a Chinese proverb but had become embellished and refined by Festing to suit his own purposes and philosophy —

'He who knows not, and knows not he knows not, is a fool. Shun him.
He who knows not, and knows he knows not, is a child. Lead him.
He who knows, but knows not he knows, is asleep. Wake him.
But he who knows, and knows he knows, is a wise man. Follow him.'

Paul Greenwood, his ADC, remembers him after dinner polishing his favourite swords with a little ball filled with powder at the end of a stick, covering himself and most of the room with powder. When he went to bed he would take two of the swords on a stand up to his bedroom. 'He was always,' recalls Greenwood, 'hoping we would be burgled so that he could try them out. As many of them were warranted to cut a man in half, some from shoulder to hip, some across the body and at least one from head to crotch, the possible consequences caused us concern. Fortunately, it never occurred.'

Festing was a man who knew the importance of style and he liked his motor cars, his officers and his dress to reflect that style. He was not always successful in this, for although he tried to start the day well polished and pressed, somehow or other he would finish the day looking bedraggled and covered with a liberal sprinkling of snuff. Paul Greenwood remembers that when Festing arrived at Eastern Command in 1954 he was extremely disappointed on finding the hearse-like Humber staff cars which had been allocated to him. One day when inspecting an Ordnance Depot, Festing came across a superannuated long black Daimler of about 1935 vintage which so delighted him he appropriated it and had it restored to life. He insisted on driving it himself and this gave rise to a series of Chaplinesque or Feydeau-like farcical scenes.

When Festing arrived at a barracks, (or indeed anywhere else) for an inspection, the receiving officer would throw open the back door with a flourish to reveal Corporal Baker, the General's driver. Hastily another member of the reception party would open the front passenger door to reveal the ADC. Meanwhile, unnoticed, in the general confusion, the General was extricating himself from the driver's seat.

So fond was the General of this car that on his promotion to the Far East in late 1956 the car was shipped out to Singapore, but after arrival in the East a vital part of the complicated transmission system failed and a replacement part had to be ordered from England. Whilst Festing was lunching with the Commander in Chief, Royal Navy, he was told that this vital part would be despatched by sea. This so annoyed the General that he ordered Greenwood, immediately after lunch to send a signal from Royal Naval HQ that the part had to be sent by air and he added: 'you must see to it that the message is sent FLASH.' Greenwood proceeded to the Navy's operations room and announced he wanted to send a Flash signal. His statement was received with consternation. Greenwood recalls 'The Officer in Charge drew me aside and said '"In the Navy we only send one signal Flash — Enemy battlefleet sighted". So our message had to be downgraded to Priority and the spare part sent by sea.'

☆ ☆ ☆

In 1956 Festing was promoted to full General and was posted to the Far East (where he was always happiest outside Northumberland), as Commander in Chief of Far East (FARELF) based from Singapore. The perceptive military correspondent of *The Observer* wrote, 'He has many Chinese and Japanese friends. On a recent visit to Indonesia he delighted his hosts by the ease with which he fitted into an Indonesian party — eating sweets, courteously passing round his snuff and towering over everyone like a genial sheepdog in an aviary.'

He always maintained that the Jesuits had the finest intelligence service in the Far East and that he could learn more from them in an hour than he could learn from any Embassy or Legation in a week. As always he was out and about everywhere and shortly after arriving in Singapore the C-in-C carried out a visit of inspection to the South Wales Borderers who were in action against the Communist terrorists in the Malayan jungle. This involved a helicopter

The Commander, Far East Land Forces, has a narrow escape, in an aircrash 1956

trip from unit to unit on the jungle edges. Festing's eldest son John and his ADC Greenwood were with him on the helicopter when just after take-off and at a height of about 300 feet the clutch connecting the main rotor blades to the engine failed and the plane plunged to the ground, the undercarriage completely collapsed and as the machine turned over each propeller blade in turn hit the ground shaking the fragile body of the machine to pieces. By a miracle the only injury suffered was a cut on the General's cheek. Greenwood was despatched to find a replacement helicopter, whilst John and the General retired to the Mess for a cup of tea. Greenwood found a replacement helicopter but could not find a pilot qualified to fly VIPs. When they boarded the relief helicopter they found the pilot going through his take-off procedure with frequent references to his operational manual — scarcely an encouraging sight. But he flew the party safely enough for the rest of the day and so ended Festing's second charmed escape from a crashed plane.

When Festing took over as Commander in Chief, Far East Land Forces in 1956 the campaign against communist insurrection in Malaya was drawing to a successful conclusion, Templer had departed to become C.I.G.S., and the war in Vietnam was just beginning to raise its ugly head. At the beginning of his tour of duty Festing took his wife, his Chief of Staff, Willy Pike (later Lieutenant General Sir William Pike), and others on a tour visiting Japan, Honolulu, Fiji, New Zealand and Australia. Festing and Pike tried to pass on to the Americans some of the lessons they had learnt — that it was, for example, of little use trying to organise on Western lines in Viet Nam, with large staffs, tanks, and specialised equipment, when what were needed were good infantry and jungle fighters — the lessons we had painfully had to learn ourselves again in Burma. The Americans, who were still technically advisers only, were sceptical and the British Ambassador Hugh Stephenson told Festing that President Diem had recently exploded publicly saying, 'the trouble with you Americans is that you have no colonial experience.'

It was of this early tour that Pike wrote, 'The thing I remember best about this tour — and indeed about all my service with Frankie — was what fun it was. He could adapt himself to all and sundry, from Prime Ministers and Commanders-in-Chief of every nationality, to private soldiers and peasants.'

Between 28th March and 24th April 1957 he undertook with his wife a tour of Vietnam, Cambodia, Hong Kong, Korea and Japan and did not lose his sense of humour or his sense of wonder as his report made plain (or as much of it as is printable).

'In Saigon we were met by a large Guard of Honour, and a minute Vietnamese General, also by Hugh Stephenson, sweating a good deal and looking even more like a toad, but it was nice to see him again. He has been a most excellent Ambassador. After luncheon at the British Embassy we visited the Headquarters of the Vietnamese Army. We then went on to the President's Palace where Hugh joined me and I then had an interview with Mr Ngo Dinh Diem. I found his French very difficult to understand as he slurs all his words together and in fact speaks it very badly. He allowed me a general conversation for about twenty-five minutes. After which he firmly focused his eye on a corner of the ceiling and talked steadily without intermission for an hour and 45 minutes. It very nearly killed me, especially as the chairs were hard — I staggered out feeling exhausted. The Palace he lives in is a very hideous affair, rather like the London North Eastern Hotel at King's Cross of about the same colour and built at the same time.

On Friday 29th March we flew to Dalat. It is a sort of French Hill Station about 150 miles from Saigon — a funny little place rather like Ceylon with a lake and lovely palm trees. We then went on and had a Vietnamese version of American briefing. Personally, I think American briefing is often rubbish, even when done by Americans. When done by somebody not American and especially someone whose command of English is poor, it verges on the comic.

On to dinner with the Minister of War. It was fun and the Vietnamese ladies could not have been more attractive or more engaging to look at. I shall always remember seeing Mary and our hostess walking down the garden together. It looked as though Mary was accompanied by a little doll, about a quarter her size.

On Saturday 30th March I paid an official call on General Maxwell Taylor at the American Headquarters and had quite an interesting talk with him and General Williams — I think in spite of the fact they live in the area they do not realise that SEATO will sooner or later have to come clean and will have to make up its mind what it really is prepared to do. The four powers in it — US, UK, Australia and New Zealand — therefore will have to decide how far they are prepared to back up their friends with actual force.

After lunch we flew to Phnom Penh and arrived at the most extraordinary place. It is now known as the Official Government Hospitality Centre and was completed a year ago as the Palace or the Official Residence for the French Commissioner-General, the last one of whom was murdered by his houseboy.

The next morning, Sunday 31st March, we went to church — I don't think I have heard a more noisy Mass. It was extremly devout and all the people who packed the church appeared very devotional, but they made a noise like a lot of cats caught in a gate. After that we returned to breakfast — We then visited Ankor Wat. It is one of the most wonderful things I have ever seen. The most striking thing to my mind is its colour, which is like a dark grey-black rock, rising out of a green sea. The scale on which it is built is something quite incredible. Ankor Wat itself is one of several temples and covers an area of 417 acres, the top of the temple is in fact the same height as Notre Dame.

After lunch — we saw another temple, Ankor Thom, which is particularly interesting because it had been left still overgrown by the jungle and here you see vast forest trees at least 200 feet high, growing out of the ruins — the place is inhabited by millions of bats with the appropriate smell.

The next day I went off to see the Cambodian Military School — It is a curious set-up in Cambodia because the Americans pay for the construction but the Cambodians prefer to be instructed by the French. I asked the American General how many of his officers spoke French and he confessed to me he did not have any.

The set-up in this country is curious. The Crown Prince was originally the King. He then decided that the two things he was really interested in were politics and saxophone playing. In order to achieve an entry into the former he abdicated in favour of his Father and Mother who are now the King and Queen. In order to achieve the latter ambition he succeeded in getting a gold and jewelled studded saxophone. He is, however, quite an intelligent fellow full of energy but has curious ways, particularly in the matter of the production of a family; most of his children being out of a marriage with his own Aunt — everyone appeared pretty happy and very friendly.[26]

26. This is a reference to Prince Sianhouk who still plays an equivocal role in Cambodia, sometimes siding with and fighting alongside the murderous Khmer Rouge of Pol Pot, and sometimes distancing himself from them. In 1979 North Vietnam "invaded or liberated" Cambodia driving Pol Pot's guerillas out of the country, but received little Western aid. In 1989 they departed, and supported by Chinese arms and money and by a surprising British and American indifference, the genocidal Pol Pot at the end of 1989 seems to be on his way back to power whilst the Cambodian Government, without medical or relief aid, has not even a seat at the United Nations to be able to protest. So the comic opera idyll of Cambodia, which had so delighted Festing soon declined into a nightmare.

In Korea I started with a visit round Imphal Camp. A vast improvement has been made since I was last here — and the standard of man management is better and I was delighted with what I saw.

In Japan everywhere one goes one is confronted with evidence of Japanese efficiency, prosperity and enterprise — I had a meeting with the late Prince Tokugawa, who would now be the Shogun had that form of Government not been done away with — He was a really most attractive gentleman — Whenever I met representatives of the late Japanese aristocracy I have always found them cultivated, intelligent and very pro-British; alas I fear their day is done.'

☆ ☆ ☆

On his tours of duty undertaken in the Far East between 1956 and and 1958, visiting every country at least twice and almost every unit in every country, his wife who generally travelled with him played an important role — defusing his outbursts of irritation, encouraging the morale of any member of his staff under attack, smoothing ruffled feathers, and being particularly kind and considerate to people he tended to ignore. She combined to a remarkable degree a Roman reserve with a feminine kindliness that made her indispensable to him as he acknowledged, although she herself did not always escape unscathed, especially when she stubbed out her cigarettes on the floor of his beloved new Rolls-Royce, purchased in Singapore and which in future years, stationed outside the Northern Counties Club in Eldon Square, Newcastle, or outside Steedman's antiquarian bookshop in Grey Street, would signal his arrival in the City.

He was acutely conscious that not to control his temper was a sin. On one occasion his ADC, to whom he had been particularly difficult, was ordered to stop the car outside a Catholic church whilst the Commander in Chief, Far East Land Forces, disappeared inside to ask for forgiveness, whilst the victim of his wrath waited for him in the car outside. And yet everyone to whom I have talked has emphasised that in spite of the upsets and traumas, the affection which Festing inspired in his staff was such that they remember their time spent working under him as the happiest and most enjoyable period of their army careers, with much laughter. 'Laughter', said General Sir Cecil Blacker, 'not because he told stories, he never did tell a funny story, but simply because of his totally individual and indeed inspired approach to the problems presented by army life.'

There was one occasion during a Cabinet meeting in Canberra, chaired by the Australian Prime Minister Menzies to which Festing had been invited to attend to discuss questions of strategic importance with the Australian Government, in the middle of which Festing needed to use the lavatory. Raising his hand like a schoolboy for permission to leave the room, Menzies gave him permission to use his private lavatory and held up the Cabinet discussion until his return. On re-entering the Cabinet room Festing with a smile on his face and in the the politest possible terms said that if he were Prime Minister of Australia he would have insisted on a mahogany rather than a plastic lavatory seat. This caused much merriment and was that evening recorded in the despatch to London. Next morning Festing noticed that his ADC Cornell had re-edited the despatch by omitting all reference to the lavatory seat. 'Why?' Festing asked, 'have you taken that out?' 'Because,' replied Cornell, 'I thought it neither relevant nor appropriate to your discussion on strategy with the Australian Government.' 'Rubbish,' came the reply, 'passages in my despatches such as that provide the best incentive for people in London to read them.' So the lavatory seat was re-edited back into the despatch.

It is said by some of Festing's detractors that he was not devoid of the defect of snobbery — few human beings are. But if there is anything in this charge he would not have regarded this as a sin for confession, but would have justified it as part of the search for quality which played such a great part in his life. Lieutenant-General Sir William Pike agrees — 'I would not think him a snob at all. He simply looked for quality regardless of rank or station.' No one had a truer or greater respect for the virtues of the ordinary man or soldier than he, and if he combined this with a naîve pleasure that at a shoot at Broadlands he was the only guest below the rank of an Earl, it showed he was only human. He did search for quality throughout his life and his shrewd assessment of those who were worth cultivating and those who were not, played some part in achieving his hugely successful career. He had long sincerely admired and had been close to Templer who was to recommend Festing to succeed him as C.I.G.S.; but there was a streak of realpolitik in this outwardly simple and bluff soldier, as when he told his ADC, Cornell: 'the way to get on in life is to make friends with people of influence who are unpopular. They will be all the more grateful for your overture of friendship, and their reports on you will reflect that. It is extremely difficult to dislike people who show they are prepared to like you.'

But the number of people he sought to cultivate or placate were few in number. If there was an amusing Rifle Brigade Major in the vicinity, he would wish to invite him to dinner to the exclusion of a General whom it was his duty rather than his pleasure to entertain. But in the end he would reluctantly accede to protests of his ADC or his Military Assistant that the General must be invited. In this and other ways his charmed circle had their work cut out to prevent him making more enemies than was wise, of people he felt did not matter. But this view that the opinions of most people did not matter was the reverse side of a self-confidence verging upon arrogance that made him such a decisive leader in Burma and elsewhere. However critical the decisions he had to take (and there were many), he never lost a night's sleep over any of them.

No one knew better than Festing the importance of not being outfaced. He loved the East, had done a great part of his soldiering there, and he believed (rightly) that he had a sympathetic insight into Oriental philosophy and attitudes that gave him an understanding of the Oriental mind unequalled by any senior serving British officer. Cornell attended him on many late drinking sessions when he proved he could drink more brandy than even the Chinese General Staff — and that is saying something. Japan appeared sufficiently frequently on his itinerary of visits, to the mystification of his staff, and Cornell found him once sitting cross-legged with a sword maker in a back street in Tokyo watching a blade being tempered and hearing something of the history of the sword.

But the most striking instance of his refusal to be outfaced was in the snow-covered hills of Panmunjom in Korea. Cornell had expected a pheasant shoot (after all, Korea is the land of the pheasant), and Festing, with South Korean senior officers to his right and left, was advancing in a straight line when a deer got up and the South Koreans yelled, "shoot, shoot." Festing did and killed the deer instantly. A South Korean officer drew his hunting knife, slit the neck of the deer and holding up his enamel army mug, drew off the best part of a pint of hot blood and handed it to Festing to drink. Festing, who was on a goodwill tour of Korea, had very little time to decide how to respond to such an unexpected invitation but, after no more than a momentary hesitation, drank the blood without a pause and without any apparent loss of composure. This example of nerve sealed Festing's reputation in senior military circles in Korea and for years was much talked about.

When in 1958 he was told of the decision that he was to be appointed Chief of the Imperial General Staff and promoted inevitably to Field Marshal, he was somewhat put out by the instinctive reaction of a member of his family: 'So now we will be able to return to live in Northumberland.'

'I have reached the very pinnacle of my profession', he said 'and is that really the only comment you can make?' He might have added 'Do you realise I am the first practising Roman Catholic to have been appointed head of the British Army since the Protestant Succession of 1688?'

8

Chief of the Imperial General Staff

Festing's reputation as a superb regimental officer and his determination to keep in the closest possible touch with the regiments so that their views could be heard through him, made him peculiarly suitable to carry into effect the revolutionary provisions of Sandys' July 1957 Defence White Paper ('The Future Organisation of the Army'). Indeed, it seems very likely that Festing was chosen to succeed Templer as C.I.G.S. primarily because he, better than anyone else, was thought capable of selling to the Army the concept of the larger regiment, an idea which was bound to be unpopular with many traditionalists. His immediate predecessor as C.I.G.S., Field Marshal Sir Gerald Templer, had, with Sandys, come to the reluctant conclusion that the administrative costs based on the single battalion regiment were too high to be acceptable for the future, and Festing on appointment was bound by this decision. Templer was an Ulster Protestant, a more conventional man than Festing but as brave and successful a leader as Festing had been. He shared Festing's devotion to history and tradition (he was virtually the creator of the Army Museum) and felt a strong attachment to the single battalion where sometimes the same soldier families had dominated the Officers' and Sergeants' messes for 200 years. He respected and knew the value of the territorial loyalty that went with it but, after much agonising, recognised that the administrative cost was too high.

Festing, although a romantic was also a realist and came to the conclusion that Templer and Sandys had been correct, and that the way ahead lay in merged brigades of larger battalions retaining as much as possible of their individuality but administered and supplied by a more centralised machinery. Many were the letters of protest he received from those affected by the reorganisation which he recognised was generally unpopular, but he hoped that a system of cross-postings within the new brigades would accelerate the promotions of the younger officers and prevent any new Ludfords arising in the future.

When Brigadier Bernard Fergusson protested, Festing replied:[27] 'It seems to me that there is a danger if in standing out for everything that one loves one may be forced to accept something which might have been avoided had a less "diehard attitude" been maintained by the Regular Infantryman. I know that this is the stock excuse for "the appeasers", but in this case having had three years of solid battling as C.I.G.S. I would ask you to believe that my attitude is dictated by a deep love for regimental tradition and not by a desire to time serve.

'I do not think it possible to run an army on a basis of each Regiment deciding for itself exactly how they propose to organise themselves. The plain fact is that there is a considerable gulf between what, for instance, the Welsh Regiments would like and what the Highland Regiments or perhaps the Green Jackets would want.

'What the Army has got to do is to produce a modus vivendi by which both types of Regiments can, within a common framework, develop efficiently and happily.'

He comforted himself that it was an inevitable continuation of the administrative standardisation policy he had initiated as Director of Weapons and Development at the War Office in 1947, and which he had continued in 1951 at SHAPE, in the interests of efficiency and value for money. In spite of his load of deskwork and his travelling overseas as C.I.G.S. he spent much time in protecting the individuality (within the merger policy agreed) of the members of the Fusilier Brigade — (the Royal Northumber-

---

27. In a letter dated 4th January 1962.

land Fusiliers, the Royal Fusiliers, and the Lancashire Fusiliers) — even down to such detail that in September 1958 Festing's application was granted that the tune "Blaydon Races", should be officially approved by the War Office as a second regimental march for the Northumberland Fusiliers.

Nevertheless, for a man of Festing's temperament it must have been with mixed feelings that he saw during his term of office as C.I.G.S. (June 1958 to October 1961), fifteen line battalions earmarked for reduction, and twenty-seven famous names disappear from the infantry order of battle altogether, and that his own beloved Rifle Brigade would disappear into the 3rd Green Jackets. He was sensitive to the charge that the Brigade of Guards had secured a privileged exemption from the larger battalion policy. Some of his greatest admirers consider that in the interest of fairness — and to rebut those who found the pill too unpleasant to swallow — he felt compelled to offer up his own regiment to lead the way and so compel all others to fall into line. And so the Rifle Brigade, 60th Rifles, and the 43rd and 52nd Oxfordshire and Buckinghamshire Light Infantry ceased to exist.

It is true that in time he won general acceptance for this policy, but there were some regiments which simply lay low and kept their heads down, and were never required to amalgamate and today still bear their original names. Since one of the main purposes of the larger regiment policy was to facilitate cross-posting to other battalions as and when they were needed, this, some feel, could have been achieved by making formal groupings of existing regiments and insisting on greater flexibility in cross-posting. But the die had been cast in 1957 and Festing had to go through with it. He once said to a close friend that the Rifle Brigade could not have chosen a worse time to have the C.I.G.S. as Colonel Commandant.

When Festing was satisfied of the importance of anything for the well-being of the army nothing was too much trouble for him and his energy was limitless. We have seen how, even when convalescing from illness in 1950, he took the unprecedented step, as President of the Regular Commissions Board, of personally interviewing every applicant for a Regular Army Commission. The trouble was that when he was satisfied that something was important only from an administrative or bureaucratic viewpoint, he flatly refused to interest himself in it. Inevitably, as C.I.G.S., the number of such matters increased proportionately to the number of matters he regarded as important. This meant either that his staff had to do what he himself should have done, or that members of his charmed circle had to stand over him and cajole him until he was compelled to do it. It was not that he was "bone idle" as was whispered in Whitehall, but that his powerful brain and imagination refused to work on matters totally without interest to him. He used to say: '99% of the jobs in this world are boring and boring people do them best.' But few men had their threshold of boredom set so low as Festing's.

Even on matters he regarded as important, he would quickly and it seemed almost instinctively, come to the correct decision and then, having made it, leave it to others to find reasons for the decision and to write it up for Whitehall. In other words, his quick grasp of what was the correct solution to any problem (which next to bravery in the field was his greatest virtue as a soldier) inverted the Staff College precept of, 'Appreciation first and solution afterwards.' He first arrived at the solution and then got bored with it and left it to his staff to write out the Appreciation. That was why he himself wrote so little and why his ADC John Cornell is able to say that: 'In the two-and-a-half years I spent with him I do not remember him writing a paper or a despatch himself of any consequence or substance. Travelling around with him I was required to carry a pocket tape recorder and at the end of every day's work, and frequently in the early hours of the morning, I was summoned to his bedroom to operate the tape recorder whilst he lay on the bed and recalled the events of the day he wished to include in the despatch, leaving it to me to knock the whole thing into an acceptable form and shape.'

There is little doubt that from the time of Festing's promotion to full General in 1956 and his posting to the Far East as Commander in Chief of Far East Forces (FARELF), Templer had Festing in mind to succeed him as C.I.G.S.

This was because, as we have seen, Templer (and Sandys) realised that Festing's popularity with the regiments made him more likely than anyone else to be able to win acceptance for the unpopular changes that the implementation of the larger battalion policy would entail.

In 1958, when Festing took over from him, Templer by general consent was considered to be with Slim the outstanding soldier of the post-war years, and people were inclined to think that Festing in comparison was much slower in intellect and generally not quite in Templer's class. General Sir Cecil Blacker, who was Festing's Military Secretary during his C.I.G.S. period and who had served under Templer, wrote: 'I soon became astonished that anyone should think this, because nothing could have been less true. Festing had a natural quickness of mind, a breadth of knowledge and an intellectual depth, which made him certainly equal to, if not superior to his predecessor. This, added to a formidable down-to-earth commonsense enabled him to get to the root of any problem however complicated.'

'The trouble was,' said General Blacker, 'that he went out of his way to conceal these attributes. The "character" which he had decided to impersonate in his later years was that of the bluff down-to-earth infantry warrior, deliberately scruffy, eccentric, caring nothing for what anyone thought of him, spending as little time as possible in the office, and as much time as possible with soldiers in the field. A lot of this was pure acting, but unfortunately it tended to fool people and as a result his general reputation as C.I.G.S. amongst the Army's intelligentsia was not as high as it should have been. I often found myself then, and since, defending him to such people out of genuine concern that his qualities were not being appreciated in Whitehall, though of course they were outside.' He was very funny when parodying others but excelled most in self parody to his own detriment.

Field Marshal Lord Carver, another unconventional product of Festing's old school, Winchester, has described[28] something of the changed atmosphere that Festing brought

28. *Out of Step*, Hutchinson 1989, pages 284-285

with him on his appointment as C.I.G.S., 'so relaxed that I often wondered if he took affairs in Whitehall seriously at all. His briefings were invariably postponed until the last possible minute and he often took little trouble to absorb them. On one occasion we were briefing him for an important meeting in 10 Downing Street about nuclear warfare. We started very late and he seemed to pay little attention. At one stage, he said: "Well, I don't know what nuclear war will be like, but, when it's all over, you'll find me dressed in sheepskins striding over the Cheviots." Cramming his papers into his briefcase and picking up his dilapidated umbrella and terrible bowler hat, he turned and said, "Gentlemen, if I thought anything was going to be decided at this meeting, I'd be as depressed as you are," and strode out.'

Whitehall exasperated him, and refusing to read the papers on a subject which bored him, relying on his quick intelligence to see him through, sometimes did not compensate for the lack of time and thought he had given it.

Where he particularly shone, aided by his capacity to get on with all sorts of people when he wanted to, was as a conciliator and negotiator. He found his Minister, Duncan Sandys, as awkward to deal with as had Templer, (Sandys was the only person who could ever make Festing feel ill at ease), but he did his best to get on with him much to the Army's benefit, although he often complained that Sandys was being "tiresome" — a favourite word of his. He got on better with the American Chiefs of Staff and the American Government than had Mountbatten, and successfully negotiated delicate matters with them, 'concealing', said General Blacker, 'under his genial, almost fuddy-duddy manner his sharp skills and adroitness of touch.'

But it was not only his adroitness which served him well. He never lost a capacity to shock Whitehall by his blunt decency and refusal to intrigue. In his autobiography[29] Marshal of the Royal Air Force Sir Dermot Boyle, then Chief of the Air Staff (C.A.S.) from 1956-59, recalls the difficulties he had with the over-adroit Duncan Sandys and

29. *My Life*, by Marshal of The Royal Air Force, Sir Dermot Boyle, G.C.B., K.V.C.O. K.B.E. A.F.C. (privately printed 1989), Pages 109-110.

Mountbatten (Chief of the Defence Staff) when both seemed to be in favour of Coastal Command being transferred from the Royal Air Force to the Royal Navy. Mountbatten had told Boyle that Sandys wanted a paper on it. 'I was very surprised,' wrote Boyle, 'that such an idea should have come unprompted into Duncan Sandys' mind. However, I told the C.D.S. that I would have the necessary papers prepared showing (as apparently we had to do about every ten years), that the case for Coastal Command staying with the Royal Air Force, was unanswerable. I did, however, feel that I had a tough fight on my hands since obviously Sandys and Mountbatten would be against me.'

'The next thing that happened', wrote Boyle, 'was that the C.I.G.S. (it was then Frankie Festing) arrived in my office one morning and was obviously furious. When I asked him what was wrong he said that he had been summoned to a special meeting either by Sandys or Mountbatten. (Those present, in addition to the convenor of the meeting, were the Chief of the Naval Staff and himself.) The Chairman announced that he had called them together to consider the future of Coastal Command. The C.I.G.S. said "Where is the C.A.S.?" He was told it was no good inviting the C.A.S. as his views on the subject were well known. Whereupon the C.I.G.S. stood up and left the meeting and said he was not going to discuss the future of Coastal Command without the C.A.S. being present — I heard no more about Coastal Command being transferred to the Navy. I mention this episode for two reasons. First, to recognise Frankie Festing's great moral courage as demonstrated in this whole episode, especially as he was new to his post and feeling his way. Secondly, the whole episode demonstrated how one honest man can completely defeat an intrigue.'

It was outside Whitehall that his assessment of personalities, aided by his ruthlessness in removing those not up to standard, made an important contribution to the well-being of the Army. General Blacker summed him up as: 'A man of real stature, an outstandingly able man of a type which now seems to be extinct in the Army and a much better C.I.G.S. than the writers of military history — the intelligentsia — will ever give him credit for; a man moreover who was immense fun to work with, although if a certain slaty look appeared in his eyes he required careful handling if a major and terrifying explosion was to be averted.'

☆ ☆ ☆

In the midst of all his world travels and inspections as C.I.G.S., he somehow found the time to write a great many surprisingly detailed and perceptive letters of advice written as Colonel Commandant of the Rifle Brigade to Rifle Brigade officers worried about their promotion prospects, and to fathers of serving Riflemen worried about the future of their sons. To one father who had not rated his son's prospects highly enough, he wrote: 'I am quite convinced he will make it. After all, one does not necessarily want too many Napoleons anyway at the same time in one regiment, nor do I regard the sort of qualities that would fit a young man for a managerial post in a commercial organisation of a go-getting variety as quite what we want, let alone want to live with.' And to another father who had rated his son's prospects of a Regular Commission in the Rifle Brigade too highly, he wrote: 'As regards the possibility of a Short Service Commission, I believe most strongly that it would be very unwise for him to consider staying with the Regiment after his application for a Regular Commission had been turned down. He would either become more and more upset that he had not been accepted as a Regular, or he might tend not to put his heart into it. Surely he would be wise to choose a career and get started as soon as possible? I am glad you felt you could write to me but sorry that I was the person who had to tell you that there is nothing that can be done.'

It was about this time too that his dress, even on the most formal parades became increasingly eccentric — rumpled and crumpled, the old darned breeches or lederhosen and tunic rarely repaired in a colour that matched the original. As Cardinal Basil Hume, Archbishop of Westminster, recalled on a visit to Ampleforth: 'He was already a Field Marshal. I was none too certain how a Field Marshal should dress, but it struck me that there was not too clear a relationship between the jacket that seemed entirely

This photograph gives some idea of why his ADC once said that sometimes on parade Festing reminded him of an unmade bed in his turn-out

conventional and the breeches that were not.' He took this as one aspect of the independent individualism of a man whose periods of retreat at Ampleforth showed what was deepest within him.

During his three years as C.I.G.S. he worked closely with Earl Mountbatten of Burma, then Chief of the Defence Staff, who admired Festing and usually got on well with him. Festing wrote of him[30] 'He had one of the most efficient brains that I have ever had occasion to work with, but I would not say it was without its complications.' One of those complications was Mountbatten's disbelief (shared by Templer) in any independent British nuclear deterrent. Festing, unlike the more intellectually agile and subtle Mountbatten, took the robust view that any accretion of strength from whatever source should not be sacrificed especially if it was under independent British command. Lord Carver quotes Festing as saying of Mountbatten: 'You see, the trouble with Dickie is that if the front door were wide open, he'd still come down through the chimney.'[31] This difference in opinion did not mar a close friendship which had begun in the grim days of 1943 in Burma and which flourished throughout the brighter fifties during shooting parties at Broadlands which Festing hugely enjoyed both as an expert shot and as an appreciative observer of a glittering social scene.

What Festing succeeded in doing was in making the army more attractive as a career. He laid great emphasis on the new six-year contract instead of three, and his period of office corresponds with some of the best recruiting figures ever achieved — 32,000 regulars recruited in 1958 and 28,000 in 1959. He succeeded in raising Sandys' figure for the new professional army from 165,000 to 180,000 with Sandys' successor as Minister of Defence, Harold Watkinson. At the same time, his insistence on the importance of maintaining an adequate "Fire Brigade", or strategic reserve to move quickly to emergencies anywhere bore fruit in the reduction of B.A.O.R. from 64,000 to 55,000 men. The work that was being done in Britain between 1958-61, though less dramatic than the reorganisation Slim had achieved in Burma, had the same object — namely, to create a greater flexibility of thought and movement — and Suez in 1956 had shown how badly it was needed.

Before Festing took over as C.I.G.S., Templer had

30. Reminiscences of Field Marshal Sir Francis Festing BS N99 quoted at page 580 of *Mountbatten* by Philip Ziegler (Collins 1985).

31. *Out of Step*, (Hutchinson, page 288).

succeeded in defeating the Communist forces in Malaya, and the army in Kenya had reduced the Mau Mau revolt to isolated acts of terrorism. Cyprus, with the appointment of Hugh Foot as Governor in 1957, had become more of a political than a military problem, and in February 1959 agreement was reached on the terms for independence. In 1958 the Middle East again became the chief preoccupation of the C.I.G.S. — the security of Jordan was threatened and at the request of the Jordan Government British troops were flown in to stabilise the situation; a similar Iraqi threat to Kuwait caused the quick assembly of a British force in the Persian Gulf. Festing's emphasis ever since his appointment, on the need for an adequate strategic reserve or "Fire Brigade", ensured that effective responses were able to be made in other troubled areas as far apart as the Emirate of Muscat and Oman, to Jamaica and in the Pacific.

Whether Festing is entitled to rank with the greatest C.I.G.S. of the recent past, such as Slim, Harding and Alanbrooke, is of course open to question. The respect which Festing inspired lay mainly with the regiments rather than with the military historians and intelligentsia in Whitehall. Incapable of hiding his likes and dislikes, relying heavily on a charmed circle of those he found amusing and avoiding those who bored him, however conscientious their work or exalted their position, he cut an idiosyncratic if impressive figure. Lieutenant General Sir John Cowley's assessment of him at the beginning of the introduction to this book perhaps sums it up and we have General Sir Cecil Blacker's view that in quickness of mind, breadth of knowledge and intellectual depth he was at least Templer's equal. As a very senior civil servant put it: 'He may not have liked Whitehall, but he dearly wanted to be C.I.G.S. — and the one is impossible without the other.'

It is interesting to note that Festing, having lobbied successfully with Watkinson to raise the Army's strength from 165,000 to 180,000, the present size of the regular army at 1st April 1988 is 158,000 men, plus 73,000 Territorials. Because Field Marshals can never retire, Festing attracted some adverse criticism when he sent a letter to every Parliamentary candidate in the country, after he had ceased to be C.I.G.S., asking whether they supported the idea of a strong Territorial Army (which was then under threat) and whether they regarded the survival of the T.A. as a political question — so that eyebrows were raised in Whitehall. They were raised even higher when he agitated by speech and by letter for the survival of the Argyle and Sutherland Highlanders as an independent regiment, doubtless to Brigadier Fergusson's delight. It can be said that in spite of the tensions generated by the "Big Regiment" policy with battalions organised on a brigade basis, he finished his tour of duty at the end of 1961 as a soldier's General, trusted by the regiments.

After retirement from the Army as C.I.G.S., his last task for the Minister of Defence was to travel to the Far East to investigate the military aspect of setting up a Unified Command there (air, naval and military). He stressed there was no technical difficulty in setting up such a command, but with five Ministries in 1962 being variously responsible for Defence matters, the quality and weight and seniority of the political advice available to the unified command was of crucial importance. Three of the five Ministries were Service Ministries and he recommenced that the Minister of Defence's overall powers should be increased to override the Services. Ministries should be strengthened to bring about a greater degree of unification into the administration of the Services. He was thanked for his efforts and recommendations and in March 1962 that was the end of his public career.

9

The End of an Era

The depth of his religious beliefs meant that Festing was entirely without racial snobbery or prejudice. He had enjoyed his soldiering in the East most of all, and his popularity with the Gurkhas, Indians and Chinese under his command was a result of the respect he felt for their own religious backgrounds.

But he demanded respect for his own as well. He always tried to keep Holy Week free for his religious devotions and avoided public engagements during that time. When Prime Minister MacMillan unexpectedly requested his attendance at the last minute at a Cabinet Committee during Holy Week he protested in words that reverberated through the corridors of Whitehall — "I am not going to allow the Prime Minister to bugger up my Holy Week" — and did not attend.

The old order was passing. In 1969 Earl Alexander of Tunis died and Festing was one of the pall-bearers. Although Festing's personality was an unusual combination of religious humility and a self assertion verging upon arrogance, his appreciation of others, like Alexander, with a very different approach to command was genuine. Festing wrote: 'He was not at all the fire-eating sort of General. There are great leaders of that sort but Lord Alexander achieved equally great leadership, without unpleasantness. He had the most charming manner, and if he asked someone to do something he invariably said "Please".'

In 1970 his old chief in Burma, Field Marshal Viscount Slim died, and again, with Field Marshal Templer and Earl Mountbatten, Festing was a pall-bearer. In 1976 Montgomery died. Again Festing was a pall-bearer but on this occasion to guard against a repetition of the comments that had been made at Slim's funeral, several guardsmen were appointed to valet him and clean up the white mildew and snuff from the cloth of his uniform and the green mould from his buttons.

He preserved his boisterous energy well into retirement. His zest for rural pursuits remained undiminished although his shooting and hunting was curtailed by an increasing arthritis which made his stick less of a theatrical and more of a sadly essential prop. In 1962 he had quite a serious fall whilst hunting. Replying to an invitation to speak at a dinner during this time he wrote: 'I am still suffering from concussion so you must see to it that I drink very little or I might say something outrageous.' Behind the facade of the Field Marshal there was, it seemed, often a small boy struggling to get out, but this defect (if it was one) ensured that this good man, unlike many other good men, was rarely dull and often very funny.

. . . And sometimes he also was profound, with a simple unfashionable wisdom. Amidst much loose talk about the futility of war he would simply say that the only truly futile war was the war you had lost, that the human race by a whisker and at great sacrifice of its bravest and best had just scraped by to achieve the right result in its major wars and so kept the way open for a civilised society, and if things had gone the wrong way the concentration camp and the gas chamber could not have been kept at arm's length from Britain.

His lack of concern for any pompous standing on dignity endeared him to all the country people of Northumberland. As in the forward positions on the Burma front, he never failed to give a cheerful greeting. A retired Lieutenant Colonel of the R.A.M.C. (Lieutenant-Colonel Boris Klukvin, a Consultant Radiologist) was early for a committee meeting in Northumberland and was filling in the time doing *The Times* crossword when a large man in a tweed suit walked into the room. 'I stood up and said "How do you do. My name is Klukvin".'

'"Festing", he said, and we shook hands. Then he sat down and produced a block of chocolate from his pocket and with a grave courtesy offered me a bite and said, "Isn't it tiresome not to be able to find time for lunch?" That was all — but quite unforgettable.'

'In his presence', echoed his Under Secretary of State at the War Office, the Rt Hon James Ramsden, 'I sometimes felt a kind of physical dazzle that was quite extraordinary.'

He was an erudite collector and student of arms and weapons, an expert on the flintlock makers and bladesmiths of Europe, on terms of friendship with dealers and collectors the world over. He was in constant correspondence with the Librarians at the Ministry of Defence, with Museum Directors and curators in charge of the Wallace Collection, and Her Majesty's Armourers in the Tower of London. When he visited friends he would invariably take with him some recently acquired chased pistols or a piece of oriental porcelain to show off — and woe betide his friends if their admiration was not thought to be sufficiently forthcoming. The extraordinary aesthetic streak that ran through the military Festings was never more vividly seen than in the case of his own father, the Brigadier General, outwardly so stiff and conventional in manner and appearance, but admired by experts as an artist of taste and imagination in *petit point.*

That noted collector and authority on antique weaponry, W. Keith Neal, has pointed out that Festing was the only non-Japanese ever to be elected to membership of the Japanese Sword Society, a tribute both to his outstanding collection and to the personal affection inspired during his visits to Japan. Neal also recalls that when Festing was appointed to the Court of the Worshipful Company of Gunmakers he would, whenever the talk bored him, pull out of his pocket a small but lethal looking pair of flintlock pistols which he would set out in front of him on the baize table of the Court to divert the discussion to a subject more to his liking. Neal also remembers how, at Boodles, Festing would sit down to lunch pistol in hand, which no waiter appeared even to notice.

As his worldly responsibilities lightened, his religion

played an even greater part in his life than before. But there are fashions in religion as in everything else, and a wise cleric once said that a Church which is wedded to the spirit of the age will be widowed in the next. What pained and angered Festing almost beyond endurance were the changes proposed in the ritual and working life of the Catholic Church, from the prohibition of the Tridentine Latin Mass to the encouragement of politicised worker priests: 'to bring the Church more in accordance with the needs and understanding of those whom it seeks to serve.'

'This is the time of the False Prophets', he often said.

In 1964, after much hesitation, he was persuaded to become a Knight of Malta. His hesitation in accepting had stemmed from a feeling that the oldest of the Orders of Chivalry, the third oldest of all the religious Orders, and by far the oldest continuously extant Lay Order in the Catholic Church, had by then become something of an anachronism. But by 1968 he had become a Knight of Obedience, bound to the daily recitation of the Rosary and to frequent attendance at Mass. Instead of the anachronism he had feared it might be, he found within the ranks of the Order the spiritual life that he had always sought with such intensity and which the Church in general was now increasingly failing to provide. He became one of the Order's most devoted members and although his advancing years prevented him from taking much part in its charitable and Hospitaller activities he was assiduous in his devotions and, within a few months of his death, attended the Order's annual retreat at Ampleforth.

Although limping badly he retained his wit and his sense of the ridiculous to the last. In October 1961 he wrote to a friend: 'I have now got two excellent hunters and I hope to have two days a week on them.' He found plenty to do; Newcastle University made him a Doctor of Civil Law in 1964; there were many City Livery dinners to attend; he was Master of the Gunmakers Company, President of the Corps of Commissionaires, a Trustee of the Sir James Knott Charitable Trust, a member of the Northern Regional Hospital Board, a member of the University Court and a member of the Board of Brixton Estates, but one cannot but feel regret that he was never given the permanent platform

In retirement, 1962, Frankie and Mary Festing

Below:
Birks, Tarset, Northumberland, the Field Marshal's home

that membership of the House of Lords would have given him, and where his robust commonsense would have graced and refreshed their Lordships' House. He confided to his son John that respect for tradition and his family would not have allowed him to accept a life peerage even if one had been offered. It would have to be a hereditary peerage or nothing and so it was nothing. But whilst he had no great wish to go to the Lords (as distinct from the contribution he would undoubtedly have made had he arrived there), a greater cause of regret with his reverence for history was that there was no offer of the Garter.

He was a passionate defender of the wide open landscape of the Northumberland of his adoption, and because great issues in the countryside often begin in the parish, he was for many years an active and assiduous member of Greystead Parish Council. When the great Kielder Dam in the North Tyne valley was first mooted he was horrified, not so much by the prospect of a great lake in the wild landscape, but by the destruction of its peace and quiet that would inevitably follow under the banner of the amenity and leisure lobbies. He was mercifully spared the knowledge that in the end the water was not urgently needed by industry after all, and that the whole scheme had been, as he would have put it 'a typical planners' cock-up.'

He directed his four sons that each should serve at least ten years in the Army and after that they could do what they wished with the rest of their lives. Two were commissioned into the Grenadier Guards and two into the Rifle Brigade. All did well enough for the Field Marshal to hope that they would all make the Army their sole career as he, his father and grandfather before him had done. He was saddened when one by one, at the completion of the ten years, each left, but regret was later mitigated by the pride he took in the success of their so different and so very surprising careers enthusing eventually over the very vocations he had so vigorously condemned — beginning with 'Impossible. No Festing ever owned a shop,' and ending with 'Yes, it's doing very well — of course it was my idea in the first place.'

Today, one is a merchant banker, another a successful portrait painter, one has made a flourishing career out of a life-long devotion to the art of the gunsmith, whilst the fourth is an art expert employed by a great auction house which considers it a bad year if he does not unearth a hitherto unknown Constable painting from some Northumbrian attic.

With a soldier's contempt for money and money-making, he gave away his collection of 120 Samurai Swords, now on loan from the donee to the Ashmolean Museum in Oxford. He suffered a heart attack and died, rosary in hand, on 3rd August 1976. Earl Mountbatten wrote: 'He was not only one of the greatest Generals I have ever had the pleasure of being associated with, he became a true friend.'

As a devout Roman Catholic, his relations with the neighbouring Anglican church at Greystead, next door to his own estate, had of necessity to be that of a friendly buttress rather than a pillar — that is to say, he supported it from the outside and wished it well in its shabby decrepitude. With entire consistency he had therefore given instructions that he wished to be "planted" near it, but not in it. So he was buried in an open field in his own ownership adjacent to Greystead church graveyard. He said that if the foxes dug him up, they had provided him with so many hours of good sport he would not grudge them theirs. Again, it was entirely consistent with his life that there was an element of the comic about this final funeral scene, with the Roman Catholic Bishop of Hexham and Newcastle in a mitre, carrying his crozier with some difficulty over a boggy corner of a field full of cow-pats and nettles, to consecrate the ground and conduct the prayers. The ceremony, with its mixture of the romantic and the incongruous, ended with the Green Jacket buglers sounding the Last Post and Reveille from a distant hill.

As Field Marshals can never retire, the War Graves Commission supplied a tombstone exactly like those in any military cemetery. This looked somewhat lonely in its isolation. It so happened that part of the graveyard wall of the church, with an iron gate in it and a cross above, was due to be demolished for the road widening thought to be essential for the hated reservoir scheme. So the graveyard wall, gate, and cross, were reconstructed and re-erected to make a walled-off graveyard plot in the field.

☆ ☆ ☆

Sir Charles Mott Radclyffe, at his Memorial Requiem Mass, said: 'Anyone who was tempted to think of him as a typical soldier sportsman would speedily find after a few hours spent in his company that behind those piercing eyes and firm mouth lay a mind enriched by a knowledge of a great many other things besides soldiering and sport; of English literature, of wine, of pictures, and above all he was the best-known and most highly regarded private collector of Japanese swords, daggers, pistols, and other weapons certainly in the United Kingdom and probably beyond. He understood quality — animate and inanimate — better than anyone I have ever known.'

☆ ☆ ☆

'The Memorial Window to Field Marshal Festing at the Royal Memorial Chapel, Sandhurst, was dedicated on 13th May 1979 and the background is the colour of the Royal Northumberland Fusiliers of which he was Colonel from 1953 to 1965, while below the Arms is the badge of the Rifle Brigade, into which he was commissioned and of which he became Colonel Commandant. At the base is shown the Divisional Sign of the 36th Division, commanded by him in Burma from 1942 to 1945, together with the insignia of a Knight of the Sovereign Military Order of Malta. At the head of the design is a representation of his favourite yacht within a laurel wreath.'